THE PHOENIX

THE PHOENIX

*From Spiritual
Emergencies to
Awareness of Self*

JEFF MALDEREZ

A. Nobody

Jeff Malderez Artist

Contents

Preface   3

To Remain   5

Part One: From Spiritual Emergencies to Spiritual
Emergence   6

   1   Introduction   7

   2   The Sacred Elephant   12

The Whirlpool   18

   3   Managing the Storm   20

   4   Recovering from Recovery   27

   5   Taking the Power back   33

A Thousand Souls Shot   48

   6   From Break-Down to Break-Through   50

I Wanna Go Home   56

   7   The Divine Balance Approach   57

   8   The Spiritual Emergence Intensity Tool   68

Part Two: From Spiritual Emergence to Awareness of Self   75

A Koan: A Student of Being   76

   9   Personal Development   78

The Key   83

10 Spiritual Integrity   84

11 The Signal   94

To Whom It May Concern   100

12 Empathy   102

13 The Art of Awareness   107

Messages   112

14 Satori Laughing (@ The Cosmic Joke)   114

Don't Listen to Me   119

15 From Aloneness to All-One-ness   121

Together as One   127

16 An Eternal Present   128

As within, so without   133

17 The Phoenix and the Magic of Rebirth   135

Referenced Publications   140

Silhouettes   141

bio.site/jeffmalderez

*Some minor edits and structure made using A.I.

First Published 2024. Jeff Malderez & A. Nobody, IngramSpark.

Paperback ISBN: 979-8-9909273-3-9
Hardback ISBN: 979-8-9909273-4-6
Ebook ISBN: 979-8-9909273-5-3

For Grandma & Grandpa...
(And for all ancestors, family, and friends as Spirit)

Thank-you Jody Morrison for your guidance, contributions and magic.

"Nobody's perfect, but who wants to be nobody?"

"You are nobody. You have no name, no form. Name and form are just on the surface. Deep down, you are just vast space. And it is beautiful - because if you were somebody, you would be limited, you would be finite, you would be an imprisoned being. No, existence doesn't allow that. It gives you the freedom of nobodiness - infinite, nonending."

Osho.

Preface

The contents of this book are not in any way meant as a substitute for professional mental health advice, support, or treatment by licensed healthcare practitioners. Whilst I have obtained an undergraduate Bachelor of Science degree in psychology and two post- graduate certificates: one in mental health groups and the other in psychological therapies, and whilst I have worked for many years in the mental health system, predominantly as a peer support mentor, I am not a licensed psychiatrist or therapist.

The following chapters, therefore, are my own personal experiences, thoughts, and theories, with input and contributions from others, on the subject of spiritual emergencies and spiritual awareness and development.

Part One of "The Phoenix" takes a scientific and analytical approach to understanding and managing spiritual emergencies. It focuses on the process of transitioning from a state of spiritual crisis to a state of spiritual emergence. Key chapters such as "The Sacred Elephant," "Managing the Storm," and "Recovering from Recovery" illustrate the methodical and practical strategies for navigating through intense spiritual experiences.

In this part, I hope to employ a left-brain analytical approach, using tools like the Spiritual Emergence Intensity Tool (SEIT) to help readers quantify and manage their spiritual experiences. This section is rooted in psychological theories and practices, providing readers with structured and logical frameworks to understand and cope with their spiritual crises. The aim here is to help readers regain control, find balance, and emerge from their spiritual emergencies with a stronger sense of self and stability.

Part Two shifts to a more intuitive, creative, and spiritual exploration of self-awareness and personal development. This section, which reflects a right-brain approach, delves into the deeper, more abstract aspects of spirituality and personal growth. Chapters like "The Art of Awareness," "Satori Laughing (@ The Cosmic

Joke)," and "From Aloneness to All- One-ness" emphasize the importance of embracing one's spiritual journey and the interconnectedness of all experiences.

In contrast to the analytical nature of Part One, Part Two focuses on the emotional, intuitive, and soulful aspects of spiritual development. It encourages readers to engage with their spiritual selves through introspection, empathy, and the acknowledgment of the divine in everyday life. This part is less about structured techniques and more about embracing the flow of spiritual growth, fostering a deeper connection with the Self and the universe.

The significant time gap between the two parts—roughly ten years—highlights a shift in what I find important to convey. Initially, the emphasis is on understanding and managing spiritual emergencies from a scientific perspective, reflecting on my professional background in psychology and mental health. In the later part, the focus transitions to a more holistic and spiritual exploration of personal development, indicating, what I hope, is a maturation in the perspective towards embracing the fullness of spiritual experiences and their emotional and intuitive dimensions.

In short, this book is meant to further the debate about spirituality in mental wellbeing as well as pose the theory that for some people, their increased awareness of their own spiritual nature and abilities to identify with Self, might lie at the root of their difficult life episodes, and not 'psychiatric conditions'.

It's time to be open and consider the possibilities free from stigma and prejudice. I invite you to join me in helping to change the current medical and social paradigm to one that embraces, as well as recognizes the meaning and value in, the spiritual dimensions and experiences of everyday life, which are, for some, at the dawning of awareness – and their realization of Self.

Jeff Malderez, 2024.

To Remain

Each to their own,
But I would call myself home.
One travels...
One looks...
One searches...

And yet;
The outward meets the inner...
I am complete.

The parts unfold...

Secret whispers...
I'm told...

To Remain.

Part One: From Spiritual Emergencies to Spiritual Emergence

Let us not look back in anger or forward in fear but around in awareness.

James Thurber

I

Introduction

If you are reading this now, then the chances are you, or someone you know, are having (or have had) a difficult time managing or coping with things on a spiritual level. On the other hand, you may simply wish to learn more about the subject of spiritual emergencies and the healing and empowerment process following their occurrence. This can be a useful exercise for not only making sense of what occurred for you at the time, but it can also serve as a useful roadmap, if you like, for guidance in your own spiritual development, growth, and awareness of Self going forward.

By re-framing past spiritual experiences away from pathologizing and stigmatizing viewpoints and labels (sadly often given to those who experience such 'episodes' by the medical establishment in terms of mental health illnesses or diagnoses,) I firmly believe one can begin to see some of these experiences for what they truly are: the minds and soul's growing awareness opening to the existence of spirit in day-to-day life.

Regardless of your motivation for reading this, I sincerely hope that these words and spiritual experiences of mine will resonate with you on a level that promotes recovery, healing, empowerment, and excitement for a more peaceful and spiritual awareness 'NOW' – all of which you carry with you long-term.

You see, recovery and healing are important first steps from any traumatic experience (which spiritual emergencies often are,) however, maintaining and paying attention to nurturing them, to allow their growth and expansion, long-term are equally important steps.

All too often I have worked with people over the years who continue to relapse into fear, paranoia, anxiety and or depression, and this breaks my heart to witness. I have been there several times to date too, so I too have the t-shirt, so-to-speak. Yet, why do we 'relapse'?

Well, I firmly believe that for some at least, what they have been experiencing is on the Transpersonal level; that is to say 'beyond the personal' – beyond the chemical, cognitive, emotional, behavioral, and physical - to that which incorporates the spiritual.

Whilst it is important to mention now, I'm not a licensed doctor or psychiatrist, I strongly feel that these people and I have relapsed due to lack of an awareness, individually and collectively, of what has been happening to us on a spiritual level, and the subsequent lack of understanding, support, and development during and following such episodes from those skilled to work with the spiritual. For as one wise person I'm honored to know once said, "Lessons not learned often get repeated".

I know first-hand and second-hand that for recovery and empowerment from any fear, paranoia, depression, or 'psychotic'-based episode to be meaningful and long term then one's approach towards healing and growth needs to be holistic and all encompassing. One simply cannot have a meaningful and sustained life in balance and health without addressing and embracing one's spiritual needs; their maturity and awareness of growth – especially if the episode was thematically spiritual in nature, as many people's transformative and painful life experiences often are.

So, what's my story? Well, when my dad suggested that I write another book, after publishing The Canary: A Journey through Psychosis, I was left feeling that I had very little else to say or add to the story of my recovery from my spiritual emergency experiences. I firmly believed I had made a full and successful recovery and that was that.

Little did I know that not only was I going to be mistaken but also that my recovery was going to have some surprising new twists and culminate in a dramatic new direction in life. Not only was I still very much in 'recovery' but I was also going to experience much deeper revelations and insights than before as well as have many more mystical experiences; all of which would ultimately motivate, inspire, and encourage me to write this book.

In December 2010, together with my ex-wife, I relocated to the USA to begin a new life in the 'Land of Opportunity.' After many months of anxiety, stress, and organization we were finally back in her homeland, and I was saying 'au revoir' for now to my family and friends back in England and to the only country I really could call 'home'.

A few months of settling in went by until one wake-up call I had which caused me to experience what I call my 'Existential Week'; or my 'Dark Night of the Soul'; or what was, in fact, yet another spiritual emergency. This wake-up call caused me, tragically, to call into question and ultimately doubt some personal foundational beliefs; the basic tenants and pillars of faith about humanity I had always firmly believed in, namely that:

1. That trying to help others is a worthwhile endeavor that can make lasting positive changes for their long-term wellbeing.

2. That doing good and striving to be a good person
is both worthwhile and meaningful.

For exactly a week I isolated myself and wrestled with these two beliefs in the hope that I would be able to hold firmly onto them. Yet it soon became obvious that I was fighting a losing battle. The more I tried to convince myself that I did, in fact, believe in them the more reasons came into my mind to doubt them.

This existential 'Dark Night of the Soul' lasted exactly a week when, to my surprise, and two miraculous 'findings' of two four-leaf clovers later, the contents of this book began to slowly emerge. My spiritual emergency had transformed once again, as it had done in The Canary: A Journey through Psychosis, into a spiritual awakening. This time, however, I was going to be transformed for the rest of my life.

For as you will discover, with each passing episode I take several steps closer to Home: my true Home, which is no country or place on Earth per-se, rather it is the awareness of my own personal spiritual nature and the connection I have with spirit as a being of light incarnated in a 'meat-suit'.

In short, I now firmly believe that probably a lot of acute mental health 'episodes', while being partly what Thomas Szasz calls a socially constructed phenomenon due to society being uncomfortable with our un-orthodox expressions of a spiritual nature in a predominately scientific and medical paradigm, is also a stage of conscious and unconscious conflict typically containing pain, suffering and searching, endured by the individual soul which just proceeds the potential for greater self-realization. This potential stage is part of a journey characterized by an inherent, unconscious, divine drive towards individuation and greater conscious acceptance of Self - the true Self – which is spirit incarnate; at One with God.

Let us open up to spirit...
'Together as One'.
Not in fear nor judgment,
Not in any religious dogma...

Rather as spirit,
Re-discovering and Re-membering
Our own true nature...

In peace, harmony, and love.

2

The Sacred Elephant

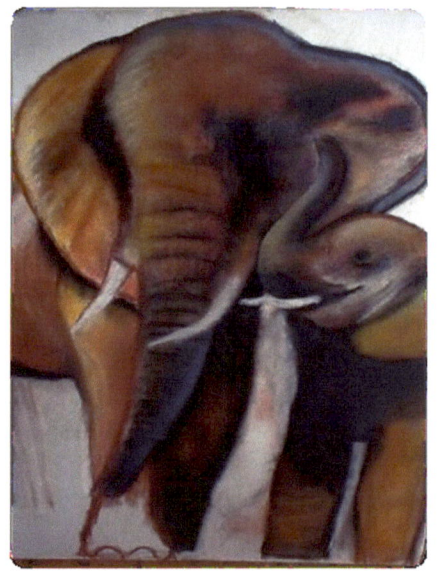

There are four questions of value in life... What is sacred? Of what is the spirit made?
What is worth living for, and what is worth dying for?
The answer to each is the same.
Only love.

Johnny Depp

I would like to start by telling you a story that my mother used to tell me when I was growing up. It takes place in India in a coffee shop where five blind men used to meet. They often used to get together and discuss many different subjects until one day their conversation turned to the subject of the sacred elephant and an intense debate ensued as to what exactly this majestic creature was. You see, none of the men had met an elephant, yet each of them had heard so much about this magnificent animal that their interests had peaked. For over an hour they debated until the eldest and wisest of the five men brought the debate to a close by suggesting:

"Clearly, we must all find an elephant and meet again here next week and share our experiences. Then we will know what an elephant is!" he pronounced.

So, off they all went to find an elephant. The first man spoke to his friend who worked at the local elephant sanctuary and arranged with her to meet the sanctuary's pride and joy: Aadidev. The following day the man went to meet his friend and have his encounter. The man was full of excitement and anticipation as Aadidev's handler led the man towards the elephant. The first blind man reached out to feel this wondrous beast.

"Ah! I understand now" he exclaimed as he wrapped his arms around the elephant's leg. He could feel it was rough like bark and wide and tall just like the trunk of a tree he thought. "The elephant is like a tree!" he concluded.

At roughly the same time in another part of the village, the second blind man had gone to the local temple to find their sacred elephant who resided there. The elephant, Kiruba, was having her lunch. The second blind man followed Kiruba's munching sounds until he found her. He reached out and found her stomach.

"Now that is interesting" he thought as he moved his hands all over Kiruba's side. "The elephant is similar to a wall" he said softly to himself.

The following day the third blind man had made the journey into the local forest where he had heard that elephants were being used to help some villagers move fallen trees. He explained to the village elder what his mission was and was led towards one elephant having a water break down by the river.

To his complete surprise the third blind man found the elephant's tail. "Excuse me" he said to the village elder, "but I wanted to feel an elephant – not this piece of old rope!" he said. The village elder chuckled and told the man that he was touching their hardest working elephant, Ramesh. The third blind man laughed and went away happy in his knowledge of this rope-like creature.

Towards the end of that week, the fourth blind man had made the journey to visit his cousin in the next village for he knew that his cousin's neighbor had a pet elephant. When he got to his cousin's home, he explained all about the coffee house discussion and about his mission. His cousin proceeded to lead the man over to his neighbor's house to visit the pet elephant Jagathi.

The neighbor led the blind man over to Jagathi and started to feed the graceful animal some coconut. The fourth blind man reached out his hand and found the elephant's tusk. He was immediately transfixed by the smoothness of the tusk and found out how sharp the point was much to his surprise! "The elephant is like a spear!" he thought to himself as he began to make the journey back to his village.

The day before the men were due to meet again back at the coffee house the oldest and wisest blind man had made the journey to meet up with a caravan traveling across the country. He knew that people in caravans often used elephants to help carry the heavy loads, you understand.

The fifth and last blind man was led up to the front of the caravan to meet Manajith – the lead elephant in the train. To say that the blind man could be heard at the back of the caravan would be an under-statement as he cried out "Oh Shiva!" and backed away in fear from the elephant's trunk. The blind man was deathly afraid of snakes you see and was convinced that the elephant was some kind of serpent! No matter how much coaxing and encouragement to have another touch of Manajith, the fifth blind man was adamant that he would never touch another elephant ever again!

And so it was that the following day all five blind men met up again back at the coffee shop where their 'elephant mission' had begun the week before.

"So" began the fifth blind man, "I think we are all agreed that the elephant is like a deadly serpent!"

The other blind men all laughed and told the oldest, and apparently wisest, blind man how very wrong he was. "It's like a tree!" exclaimed the first blind man. "No, no, no, don't you mean a wall?" said the second blind man. "Ridiculous!" said the fourth blind man, "you mean a spear!"

"You are all wrong" said the third blind man softly, "the elephant is just like a piece of rope" he said with conviction.

Just like the week before another heated debate ensued which lasted long into the evening. Each blind man had believed so strongly in their experience that neither man was willing to really listen and accept the others' story as being meaningful or worth listening to because of the encounters' extreme differences. And so, they left the coffee house without reaching an agreement on what the sacred elephant creature truly was.

Whilst my mother used to apply the story of the five blind men and the elephant to her profession as a mentor for teacher trainers in adult education, I feel that its powerful message can be applied to so many different aspects in life as well as to some of the greatest mysteries in life itself.

In short, we all have very relevant pieces of the puzzle – and in my case, relevant pieces of understanding and degrees of awareness of the spiritual emergence process as well as meaningful and hopefully useful approaches and strategies along the path to recovery, empowerment, and growth in awareness of Self.

I am but one voice with my own experiences, thoughts, theories, and insights. Yet I have tried to be mindful of this fact both in terms of the language I use as well as with the metaphors, symbols, and diagrams I have used in this book so that a greater number of people can relate to and connect with what I am saying and describing.

Experience contains so much more than words can often convey. However, I really and truly hope that on some level you can resonate not only cognitively or intellectually with what I'm saying but also in your felt experiences in life as well as with your feelings of the heart and soul. For I firmly believe that:

Knowledge becomes wisdom when it is personal experience.

In summary, it is together we can fully understand, heal, empower, and expand our individual awareness for the benefit humanity as a whole. I hope to do my part and I invite you to read and reflect on how my experiences fit into your understanding and your developing wisdom of the magnificent and sacred elephant that is your life experience as well as our collective experience of reality itself.

The Whirlpool

Gasping for,
And drowning in,
Spiritual air...

I send out
My distress flare...

Hoping in,
And praying for...
Another miracle to come my way.

I reach out,
Eyes upon the shore...
I can't swim,
Not anymore.

The outward becomes the inner,
As I fuse...
With this deluge,
And hit rock bottom.

In this moment
All about me is light...

Penetrating the cracks
Of my darkened heart...

From which the phoenix is born.

3

Managing the Storm

Make no mistake about it – enlightenment is a destructive process.
It has nothing to do with becoming better or happier.
Enlightenment is the crumbling away of untruth.
It's seeing through the façade of pretense.
It's the complete eradication of everything we know to be true.

Adyashanti

The notion of perception of reality plays a pivotal role for many people because it is most often the medical establishment which steps in when one is having a difficult time with things. This is often very true also for those people experiencing difficult spiritual emergence experiences. All too often, these individuals will be diagnosed with an 'illness'– called psychosis (of one form or another.) I am no different, yet as you will discover, a new way of thinking and approaching this is available to you.

Before we look at this new approach to these experiences, let us first examine the typical biological approach to psychosis and its definition. Psychosis stems from the Greek word 'psyche' meaning soul, and 'osis' meaning abnormal condition – roughly speaking. Most definitions of psychosis will state that the individual will be experiencing a variety of symptoms, most often including perceptual hallucinations, delusions and a 'loss of touch with reality.'

The typical western medical model for psychosis is one which tends to pathologize the condition and describe it as a disease of the mind. Western psychiatry points to the neurophysiologic evidence relating to the dopamine system of the brain which, in the case of psychosis, tends to be producing too much of the neurotransmitter. This Dopamine Theory of Psychosis has paved the way to the development of the anti-psychotic medications called typical and atypical antipsychotics which block the D2 dopamine receptors in the brain's dopamine pathways. These medications which are hoped to suppress the symptoms of psychosis are the primary treatment for psychosis in the western world.

What is uncertain, however, is whether this overproduction of dopamine in the brain is a reactive or causal symptom of the psychotic state. Moreover, it raises vital points in the definition which are being assumed by the mental health system and those within it.

Namely that, who has the right to judge and say that what one person sees, hears, feels, or believes is occurring for them is nothing more than a symptom of a diseased mind and that they have 'lost touch with reality?' Whose reality are we talking about anyway? Refer to the Sacred Elephant for a moment.

As a winner of the Royal College of Psychiatry essay prize in 2006, Dr. Nicki Crowley expands on this point in her winning paper 'Psychosis or Spiritual Emergence? - Consideration of the Transpersonal Perspective within Psychiatry:

> Psychotic phenomena such as delusions and hallucinations, described and classified in ICD10 and DSM IV, follow clinical observations, which in western society are understood as symptoms of illness. This is based on the assumption that we understand the nature of 'reality', and that there is a narrow band of 'normal' perception, outside of which there is little useful potential. (Crowley, 2006: 1)

I submit by making the assumptions, diagnosing, and prescribing 'treatment' is all done solely on the grounds that they know 'reality' better than you do and on judging what you are experiencing as being essentially 'useless' and without meaning. How rude – and how patronizing is that? Have they had your experiences? Can they read your mind and feel your heart? Have they walked in your shoes? I would argue not. What part of the elephant are they experiencing? Okay, maybe not your part, but that no less invalidates YOUR experiences. No one part of the elephant is more encompassing or more meaningful than another.

Moreover, I would submit to you that in most cases, your difficulty in coping is not really being helped; rather your unwanted behavior, ideas and beliefs are being suppressed and made to go away – all based on individuals' and a system's approach which believe they 'know reality' better than anyone else and makes you comply to their definition – either forcibly or otherwise.

Lastly, I would also submit that for most cases, those people who mention anything at all spiritual in nature will be judged according to a 'narrow band of perception' of reality, by a medical system which does not accept the spiritual by and large, and by people who have never had such experiences themselves.

Surely, this is wrong and another more accepting, non-judgmental, more caring and supportive approach is required which will accept the spiritual – with those who themselves have gone through similar experiences. Enter the field of Transpersonal Psychology.

Here the term transpersonal means to transcend or 'go above' the personal realms and ego-boundaries to one which incorporates the spiritual aspects and dimensions of the higher Self, and in Crowley's (2006: 1) terms, that are stages of "psychological growth or consciousness that move beyond the rational and precede the mystical."

The model Crowley considers for those people that might be label as being 'psychotic', are spiritual emergence or spiritual emergency, depending on how the individual assimilates the experience. This model incorporates these extrasensory symptoms and has been influenced by a great many disciplines, ranging from experimental psychology to anthropology to consciousness research and even to mythology. This model was originally coined by the husband-and-wife team Stanislav & Cristina Grof who founded the American Spiritual Emergency Network at the Esalen Institute in 1980, a foundation still very much in existence today.

Going back, the term 'transpersonal' was associated with a distinct school in the humanistic psychology movement in the 1960's. In 1969, Abraham Maslow and Stanislav Grof, among others, initiated the 1st issue of The Journal of Transpersonal Psychology, and in 1972 the Association for Transpersonal Psychology (ATP) was established.

Many people have sought to define transpersonal psychology, and many definitions exist. Some include:

> *Transpersonal psychology is concerned with the study of human-ity's highest potential, and with the recognition, understanding, and realization of unitive, spiritual, and transcendent states of conscious-ness.* (Lajoie & Shapiro,1992:91)

Transpersonal psychology affirms this movement of spiritual seeking and places the highest value on the realisation of our spiritual nature. Spiritual experience is viewed as desirable and spiritual seeking is seen as natural, healthy, and, in the final analysis, the only truly fulfilling answer to the challenge of existence. (Cortright, 1997:158)

The most exhaustive study, that I've found, of all the definitions was conducted by Lajoie and Shapiro (1992:90) who reviewed forty definitions of transpersonal psychology that had appeared in literature over the period 1969 to 1991. They found that five key themes featured prominently in these definitions:

1. states of consciousness,
2. higher or ultimate potential,
3. beyond the ego or personal self,
4. transcendence,
5. and the spiritual.

Yet, the definition which most resonates with my experiences, and illuminates why modern western psychiatry's narrow band of percep-tion has a limited grasp of reality, is Walsh & Vaughan's (1993) defini-tion of the experiences themselves:

> *Transpersonal experiences may be defined as experiences in which thesense of identity of self extends beyond (trans) the individual or*

personal toencompass wider aspects of humankind, life, psyche or cosmos. (Walsh & Vaughan, 1993: 203)

So, what is spiritual emergency and how does transpersonal psychology define and differentiate it from spiritual emergence? Well, let us turn to the founders of the term for a definition and an explanation. The Grofs (1990), in their book The Search for the Stormy Self, define the spiritual emergence process in terms of a movement that an individual takes towards a greater and expanded way of being that involves a deeper connection with other people, and with nature and with the cosmos. They also point out that it is usually also accompanied by a greater amount of emotional and psychosomatic health.

Lastly, lastly make the point that spiritual emergence is an innate characteristic for all of us and that our capacity for spiritual growth is as natural as biological growth.

In short, the process of spiritual emergence can be likened to a spiritual veil being lifted from consciousness or awareness that is a natural and healthy part of human life.

However, for some people this process can take them by surprise or erupt so forcibly that their day-to-day functioning can be disturbed. At this point a spiritual emergence becomes a spiritual emergency.

I have experienced several incidences of spiritual emergency that at their core, all shared similar themes and motifs. The definition that I most closely relate to is again offered by the Grofs (1990):

> *Spiritual Emergencies can be defined as critical and experientially difficult stages of a profound psychological transformation that involves one's entire being. They take the form of non-ordinary states of consciousness and involve intense emotions, visions and other sensory changes, and unusual thoughts, as well as various physical*

manifestations. These episodes often revolve around spiritual themes: they include sequences of psychological death and rebirth, experiences that seem to be like memories from previous lifetimes, feelings of oneness with the universe, encounters with various mythological beings, and other similar motifs. (Grof & Grof, 1990: 37-38)

Each of the episodes I have had follow not only similar structures; they also have similar themes, occurrences, and outcomes. I have had, to date, five major acute 'episodes', all of which began with elation and a profound sense of being in-touch with spirit and the divine. The duration of this phase was roughly the same for each episode, lasting roughly a few weeks to a month. Following this phase, I then experienced a dramatic and overwhelming crash into the darkness of paranoia, fear, and terror. Yet, with each episode the duration of the journey back into the light became easier and faster.

One would now think that by and large I had successfully navigated back to dry land and my healing and recovery was complete. However, for as we will see in the next chapter, this was far from the truth as a new set of challenges lay before me.

4

Recovering from Recovery

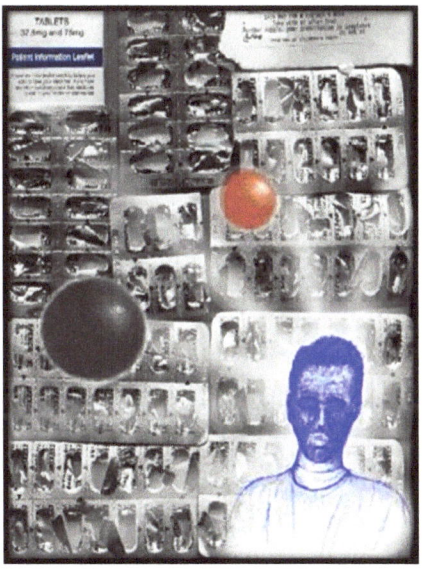

The truth you believe and cling to, makes you unavailable to hear anything new.

Pema Chodron

Many people talk about recovery following a traumatic or painful life event or episode – as spiritual emergencies or powerful instances of opening one's awareness up to spirit can be - and yet recovery itself can bring on its own issues and problems for one to deal with long after the episode has subsided. All too often this stems from the exposure to, and acceptance of, what the medical profession, your family or peers, or society at large has described your experience away as being – often out of ignorance, misinterpretation, misdiagnosis or even fear of what they are seeing or witnessing in you. Medications and other 'treatments' to halt the episode's symptoms are 'prescribed' and psychiatric labels are sometimes 'given'. But what if it is YOU who is responsible for treating yourself this way? What then?

While some people might benefit – especially in the acute phase of their episode – from taking certain types of medications, I strongly feel that if more attention was paid to their spiritual needs and development during and following their episode, then less people will relapse back into fear and paranoia again in the future as I did.

Let us now begin to start to re-address this imbalance by examining some of the issues faced within oneself following a spiritual emergency episode, beginning with how I almost bought into – hook-line-and-sinker – my mental health past. I still, to date, take medication, and yet I have come to realize that my need to take certain medications no more defines me than the scar on my face, or my sub-dislocating shoulder that pops out from time to time, nor any other part of my 'meat-suit'. I am beginning to come to terms with the fact that my being – on a spirit and soul level, more closely resembles who and what I am – and, without meaning to sound immodest – is in ok shape.

And yet, all too often we live in a world where our minds and bodies take precedence and our spirit or soul left by the wayside. Is it any wonder, therefore, when our spirit side steps in to take control of the helm for a while, shakes you to the core, and says:

"Oi – look at me! Why won't you pay attention to MY needs and development?!"

For me, at any rate, it is a given that we are all made up of soul, mind and body which closely interact with one another on many different levels, but we are also all expression of spirit and those who choose to communicate with, or those who expresses their own spiritual nature, however they are urged to do so, (without harming themselves or others of course,) need support in coming to terms with what happens for them during their spiritual emergence episodes; with accepting and letting the fear and paranoia go; in helping to develop their abilities and/or gifts; and with guidance in being safe and balanced throughout. I know for sure I needed all of these things, and still do.

For those people who have been affected by the mental health system of labels, diagnoses, 'treatment' and medication – a whole host of symptoms or reactions towards our interaction with the said system can occur. This can hamper our 'recovery' in a very real sense in many ways. Let us now examine a few of these that many have, and do, face.

Acceptance and 'Letting go'

As a man, admitting any weakness or 'flaw' in oneself can be an extremely difficult thing to do at times. In my case, the evidence seems to be there that medication helps to stabilize certain brain chemistry for me to manage in a healthy way. The facts appear to be there as without the medication I experience very severe and fearful 'episodes'.

Therefore, a chemical imbalance in my brain is one issue I face and accept it I must. Yet, let it define me and consume me completely, I will not.

For as we shall see later, some 'flaws' or 'cracks' are not only beautiful but can also be, at times, a gift. To date, for example, I have used my past experiences in this area, and how I managed them, as well as how I worked with them, to help many others cope, and move through, their own spiritual emergency experiences.

Quite often, these gifts are uncovered in people, I now believe, who, at the time, required them as a learning experience, to train them, by experience, to help re-enable and re-empower others in similar situations, as true peers. Yet as with all gifts, however, you may grow out of them in time, or they might be taken away from you. So, the process of accepting that and 'letting go' of them is of paramount importance.

I know from personal experience that during some of the most extreme states I found myself in, much of what occurred for me was thrilling and uplifting and I did not want to go away or end. Inevitably, however, the acute phase subsided, and I found it very emotionally difficult to accept that and let go of being in that spiritually connected state as it was so emotionally powerful for me. I used to get angry and wished I was back in that state once more, feeling the emotions I felt and experiencing the thoughts and connections as I had done before.

Like with old Christmas presents from your childhood, past gifts can remain strongly in your mind for years to come. However, the time comes, inevitably, when that little boy or girl out grows their toy and sometimes the magical experiences and gifts given during acute phases of spiritual awakenings must also be 'let go' of in order that you can carry on your path in life and experience the next lesson to learn. This being said, and as we shall see, 'letting go' does not necessarily mean that they disappear altogether.

Moving Forward

This process of accepting and 'letting go' I now believe, is necessary in order to move forward in life in a positive and healthy manner. Yet, life and awareness is not a race; it takes the time it takes for us as individuals to learn this. Moreover, what has happened has happened, you can't change the past. What you also cannot do is wish to 'go back' to how you were either before an episode, or even during. Your past experiences have made you who you are today, and you have changed as a result in many ways, I dare say, stronger and more insightful as a result despite the fear and the elation that might have occurred.

Of course, the hardest part of this is to know and really feel that this is true. Childhood gifts are one thing, spiritual gifts, on the other hand, are something quite different. They, perhaps, touch us on a deeper level than material gifts and so emotionally are more difficult to let go. All I can say is that with my past spiritual gifts, the process of letting go was one of a belief in the process itself; and that was good and for the best.

And yet, in my experience at least, the process of 'letting go' has resulted in their further development in a more mentally healthy and stable manner! I believe by my letting go of them in the past I've 'freed up' my mind to focus more intensely in the present: the 'Now', and with each passing 'Now', I'm continually discovering that I did not lose any-thing of the gift itself, rather only the 'locked-in' or 'fossilized' emotive memory and experience of it.

In other words, what I'm doing more of these days is to consciously practice 'freeing-up' each passing present moment of emotional 'bag-gage' or holding on to the past, for further gifts and their development for me Now. If one is weighed down heavily in the past with emotional baggage, then one cannot, in my opinion, be fully in the present. For in my experience, it's in the present that miracles and gifts can and do occur. Focus on the past, and you will miss them.

Yet, for those engaged in the mental health system, perhaps the greatest obstacle in one's 'recovery', one could argue, occurs on a wider societal level. Persistent and persuasive stigma, ignorance, and misconceptions (in my experience) from western society's attitude towards people's difficult spiritual experiences to this day sadly still occur. Let us now turn our attention towards helping address, re-balance and go some ways towards healing this situation.

5

Taking the Power back

*And those who were seen dancing were thought to be insane by
those who could not hear the music.*

Friedrich Nietzsche

I am passionate about those people affected by the field of mental health for not only did I engage with services during many of my spiritual emergence episodes but have also worked in the industry helping those people heal and maintain their well-being, whilst at the same time trying to maintain my own mental health.

I now strongly feel things need improving and that sadly all too often people are sometimes wrongly diagnosed with mental health conditions when in fact are really experiencing episodes of opening to spirit and the Self. This can produce a whole new set of obstacles for the individual concerned that is, in my opinion, spurred on by what I call the western, so-called, 'developed' societal attitude malfunction - the roots of which lie in the reigning current paradigm of psychiatry.

The notion of empowerment for mental health service-users is critical, I feel, in this whole dilemma, and whilst it is currently enjoying a lot of debate in the field within 'developed' societies around the World and is often at the heart of discussions about recovery, more needs to change. I strongly feel that if we are truly passionate about helping people recover, in whatever terms that word means to them, from traumatic or distressing life episodes, then we must do what we can to enable people using services to feel re-empowered again and do what we can for them to be taken seriously.

In this chapter I propose that to help the collaborative process of empowering service- users, the notion of power within the mental health systems and societal attitudes towards mental health 'conditions' both need addressing. Moreover, I suggest that a fundamental barrier against empowerment for service-users still, sadly, lies in an alarmingly and potentially damaging imbalance of power within mental health services in these societies caused by a societal attitude malfunction which needs immediate healing.

While this is a relatively lengthy chapter, I sincerely hope you find it informative and thought-provoking, if nothing else. What I ultimately hope is that it may enable or motivate you to help all of us to make a real difference for the better; to know you are not alone; and go some ways to normalizing your spiritual experiences despite any mental health 'label' or diagnosis you might have been given.

All of this having been said, do your own research as well so as to form your own informed opinion. Don't just take my word for it, for the information and evidence is out there.

The 'Developed' Societal Attitude Malfunction

Let me start by introducing to you the late Hungarian-born psychiatrist, Professor Dr. Thomas Szasz. Dr. Szasz often spoke out against his own profession, that of psychiatry, and its harmful and stigmatizing methods for 'treating' people with mental health conditions. In one lecture given to the Citizens Commission on Human Rights International (2006), he went so far to say that the profession has indeed made-up or created labels of mental health dis-eases, which really have no basis in scientific evidence or research.

Bogus or pseudo-scientific mental health diseases, like Drapetomania (which was a legitimate diagnosis for slaves who had fled their captors) or Hysteria (the diagnosis given to menopausal women), as described by Thomas Szasz in his lecture, are fundamentally based on no objective scientific evidence and are often culturally and generationally specific. They are, therefore, not really grounded in any biological malfunction but rather in a societal attitude malfunction which is heavily dependent on the timeframe or era and the culture or society the behavior is being observed in.

Obviously, what with the advancements in medical technology and research, it is very understandable that more mental health conditions with genuine biological, neurological or genetic causes have been discovered since Thomas Szasz's time studying psychiatry. Yet, I question the extent to which and how his original 6 or 7 mental health conditions he studied back when he said he was training have legitimately and reasonably escalated to the hundreds we have now – all within a time frame of approximately 90 years or so.

I feel that a few of our current 'legitimate' mental health conditions or diseases, like ADHD as pointed out by Szasz, incidentally, are nothing more than a desperate attempt by society's reigning paradigm, spurred on by the resulting societal attitude malfunction, to try and explain and 'treat' the unexplainable and 'untreatable' with current psychiatric methods and theories.

I now also believe that what I went through, spiritual emergencies, falls into this category. I will explain why I think this is so later in the chapter, but first I want to look at how we got to this situation and go some way towards understanding the current balance of power within psychiatry, its impact on service-users and what I mean by the societal attitude malfunction in more depth.

The observed 'abnormal' behaviors, which are believed to be caused by these so-called mental health diseases, seem to frighten society, I would suggest, because it simply does not understand them. The resulting knee-jerk reaction to this is to try and explain the behavior it finds upsetting or distressing to find ways and means to make those behaviors is, in fact, the 'sane' others or the 'sane' society here which has the issues and problems which need addressing – and often not the patient.

These bogus diagnoses are, at best, a very dubious attempt to try and explain these behaviors, based on assumptions and hypotheses (theories, in effect) which are not grounded in any objective scientific evidence, and then which try to 'treat' or 'cure' those behaviors by saying that what it is doing is in the 'best interests' of the patient. Or, at worst, these bogus diagnoses are a covert or an overt attempt to put in place controlling mechanisms to try and 'normalize' or 'pacify' behaviors for which society, and often not actually the patient them-selves, finds distressing or upsetting or hard to handle and manage or simply understand.

In short, the offending society tries to justify and rationalize its oppressive actions in terms of what it believes is 'best' for the patient when, in fact, it knows, either implicitly or explicitly, it is simply choosing to push the 'problem' away or underground and not face what it doesn't understand.

In fact, I would go so far as to say that society is frightened of what these behaviors represent in itself, and it simply can't handle that fact. It takes the easy way out without acknowledging its role in it or by accepting its own responsibilities for it. As I understand him, Thomas Szasz even goes so far as to say that society itself causes or at the very least, fabricates these mental health 'myths', to justify its controlling mechanism of that which it cannot handle or accept or finds threatening.

If this is the case, and I believe there is some evidence to suggest that this is so, then shame on society. Us citizens and members of society who happen to undergo changes in consciousness are no less members of society and expect the same equality and human rights than those other members of society who do not experience what we do. Accep-tance of and a lack of stigma towards people who suffer from organic problems and diseases highlights society's attitude malfunction clearly here when comparing its attitude towards people in different mental states than the 'norm'.

So, a biological difference in the 'norm' is a valid and accepted and tolerated difference while a difference in behavior or conscious state is not. Whichever way you look at it: it's discrimination, pure and simple.

It's time to change this injustice. Together we all make up society and it is together we can make a difference. Even your thoughts and behavior, YES YOURS, could make a huge difference to help change societal attitudes. You could be the one who is at the tipping point that creates a paradigm shift in societal attitudes, behavior, and acceptance of difference. It's only a matter of numbers and of critical mass I believe. It's time to heal society. Help us to heal society's attitude malfunction for the benefit of all of us: patients and non-patients alike. I believe we all would be much richer for it.

I highlight the issue of this societal attitude malfunction in my book The Canary: A Journey through Psychosis. I refer to the fact that some African tribal cultures are far less willing to stigmatize and judge the patient's behavior as being merely 'crazy' and without real meaning for them, but choose, instead, to adopt a rather enlightened attitude of seeing what their society as a whole can learn from the patient's behaviors.

In fact, on a scientific, evidence-based, note about outcomes and recovery for mental health patients, it is interesting to note that some research in this area indicates that it is often 'developing' countries and not 'developed' countries that are producing the best 'outcomes' for recovery. One such study which suggests this was conducted by the World Health Organisation:

Jablensky, A., Sartorius, N., Ernberg, G., Anker, M., Korten, A., Cooper, J. E.,Day, R., and Bertelsen, A. (1992). "Schizophrenia: Manifestations, Incidence and Course in Different Cultures. A World Health Organization Ten-Country Study." Psychological Medicine Monograph Supplement, 20. Cambridge: Cambridge University Press.

The seemingly more 'under-developed' or 'less evolved' societies around the World appear to be doing something right and are probably far more evolved and wiser in how it learns from and adapts to and assimilates changes and differences within its population than we do in 'developed' societies. Certainly, food for thought here I feel.

Taking the Power Back

All of this inevitably raises the notion of power, which is of paramount importance with this issue. When looking at the notion of power within this context, at least two main factors come into play:

1. Who societies view as being worthy to wield power and deserve an 'authority' status on a particular subject;
2. The degree to which we, as individuals, believe that we have the power to control events and situations (and therefore, one could argue, our mental health state) which affects us.

It should be fairly obvious that when looking at the current state of affairs within 'developed' societies that most of the power and authority is given to professional individuals (such as psychiatrists and other mental health professionals) and groups or organizations that are affiliated with science, such as government 'think-tanks', peer-reviewed research studies published in journals, and, of course, the pharmaceutical companies, to name just a few.

This is largely the situation because the current reigning paradigm within mental health is still very much based in science and the scientific method which includes research.

While the issues of nature versus nurture and cause and effect are still very much up for debate it is still assumed that science will produce most of the answers (and will, no doubt, inevitably involve something to do with neurotransmitters in the brain or some other biological mechanisms, such as genes.)

However, like times gone before, paradigms do and will shift and change. Hundreds of years ago it was religion that was the dominating paradigm and, as such, it was often the clerics and scholars who wielded most of the power then. Whomever controls power plays a pivotal role in shaping how society views differences between individuals – no more so than when looking at the issue of mental health.

Back then, for example, 'voice hearers' or people who reported to have had communication with something of a spiritual or religious nature would have been treated very differently to how they are treated today. I need not mention that if Jesus, Mohammed, Buddha, and all of the prophets and apostles of all the various denominations and religions were to speak and behave like they did back then in today's 'developed' societies, most, if not all, of them would be diagnosed with some kind of mental health condition and be subjected to 'treatment'.

Obviously, this is a very sensitive topic for debate, and I appreciate societies' issues and problems with people going so far as to claim that they are the 'second coming' and other similar claims. However, these types of spiritual experiences that even the apostles and followers of these religious leaders and figures reported to have had still get reported to this day. Many people who I have worked with over my many years working in this field report what would not be out of place from something in Revelations in The Bible or from something in other similar holy books and manuscripts.

The point is while the paradigm has changed over the years the types of experiences many people go through, I dare say, have not. In order for all of us who have experienced some kind of spiritual experience to start to re-gain some of our power back, it is first necessary to understand how the power system is currently balanced out. I hope I have provided some of the basics here and, as you can see, it is far from an even balance.

So, what can we do practically to help re-address this imbalance and reclaim some of our power back? Well, I would say that the second main factor, when looking at the issue of power within a mental health context, can help us enormously here. While great work is being done by service-user groups and the whole service-user and peer movement in general, I would add that we, as individuals, can do a lot as well.

I'm talking about the extent to which we believe we have the power to affect events and situations that affect us. Rotter (1954) postulated the concept of the Locus of Control in his social learning theory of personalities which explains what I mean here quite well. Put simply, people with a greater internal locus of control believe that their own behavior and actions have a large effect on events and situations which affect them. Conversely, people with a lesser internal locus of control believe that powerful others, fate, or chance, largely control events and situations which affect them.

While looking at this notion from a mental health point of view many of you might say that we have very little control over what our psychiatrists and mental health professionals diagnose us with or prescribe to us. It's merely cause and effect, one might say. They are only consulting the DSM-V (or the Diagnostic Statistical Manual Version V used in the USA) or ICD-10 (the International Classification of Diseases version 10 used in Europe) and applying the relevant medication to that category or diagnosis.

I would like to add, however, that psychiatrists are still people and therefore are still subject to the same bias and a whole host of other subjective influences like past experiences and assumptions and prejudices etc, as we all are, and, as such, will not be judging your behavior and speech purely from an objective standpoint when consulting these diagnostic manuals.

However, if we were able to work on increasing our internal locus of control to the point where we could see and understand the connections with and the effects of our own behavior and actions on the events and situations we find ourselves in, then we could choose to change how we perceive them, and perhaps, more importantly therefore, how we feel and think about them. In short, we could manage our own mental state from situation to situation rather than feeling that they control and dictate to us how we should or ought to feel and think. Not only that, but by seeing the relationship clearly, we could, in effect, create our own healthier realities.

While this idea might sound fanciful and quite far out there for some, it also sounds logically achievable and worthwhile pursuing I feel. Some Buddhist traditions and ways of viewing the World, for example, stem from a similar kind of belief. So, many people do and actively attempt to achieve this.

Now, I want to leave this idea with a final thought. It's about language and its relation to and impact upon identity, and ultimately therefore our sense of self. Sadly, too often I meet service-users who have bought into the label of their diagnosis to such an extent that they find it very difficult to describe themselves in any other way: 'I have psychosis, or I am a psychotic. I am a service-user survivor or other similar terminology' and go on to describe their personality or character in terms that often refer in some way to the symptoms of their label or diagnosis.

While diagnoses can be helpful for some (for understanding their condition better and choosing possible helpful 'treatments' and for helping their family and friends to understand them deeper etc.) it can be very damaging also. For some people their label (which has been given to them by those in society with the current 'power') consumes them to such an extent that it forms the very basis and core component of how they view themselves at the virtual exclusion of all the other facets that make up who they really are. Sadly, I am not making this up.

Through years of possible conditioning by the mental health system and by societies' attitude malfunction and through possible reliance on and institutionalization within the system resulting in a degree of learned helplessness, some people have lost their power to such an extent that they have unwittingly allowed those currently in authority, through the use of labels and diagnoses amongst other things, to undermine their own power of self-definition and therefore their sense of identity. This is a ghastly thing to witness, something which no one should ever have the right or that much power to do.

Like Al Pacino's character in the film Scent of a Woman said: 'There is nothing quite like the sight of a broken spirit.' That is exactly how I feel when I try my best to help those people I work with re-gain their lost power. It can be utterly soul-destroying at times; the power balance must change.

Spiritual Emergencies

Let us now turn our attention to how spiritual emergencies fit into this whole picture. I now believe that all of the issues discussed above are very relevant, no more so in fact, than when looking at the topic of spiritual emergencies. The prevalence of the 'developed' societal attitude malfunction and the imbalance of power are both extremely evident when looking at how people who report spiritual emergence experiences are often treated by the mental health system and by the 'developed' society at large. One only has to look in the media, or the language people use, especially in relation to implied insults like: 'Have you taken your meds today?' to see what I mean here. I'm sure you can think of many more examples.

While spiritual emergencies can include 'hallucinations' or alterations of any of the senses as well as possibly voice hearing, I would like to focus our discussion on 'delusions' or the abnormal, strange or alternative beliefs component. The reason for this is because a set of beliefs cannot solely, I believe, be attributed down to malfunctions or abnormalities in anything purely biological or physiological, like neurotransmitters or genes. They involve a person's mind and conscious state and personal experiences which go beyond merely that which is only felt and perceived by the body and by its senses.

I also would like to focus on the issue of 'delusions' because it is often with these types of beliefs that those in power and society at large have the most problems with and find hard to handle, especially in relation to people experiencing spiritual emergence episodes.

After my own research in this area and with my experience of working in adult mental health, I have come to believe that probably throughout the ages, from the time of Jesus and before, right up until the modern day, people all over the World have gone through these types of experiences. The differences between how they are treated depended entirely on the dominant paradigm in that society and, therefore, who held most of the power, as well as the time frame they were being observed in. Back then, they were listened to and respected. Now people are stigmatized and thought of as 'crazy' and their beliefs are judged to be without any sense or meaning. I guess we are just unlucky with the timeframe and society we have been born or live in.

However, that being said, the current people in power are probably out of touch with the 'sane' person on the street if they believe that these types of beliefs are, in fact, 'abnormal'. For as one study cited in a paper by Rufus May (2010) points out:

> *Commonality of alternative beliefs Studies have shown that all sorts of beliefs [a] Psychiatric professional might see as irrational including beliefs in magic, aliens, telepathy and spiritualist beliefs are extremely common in the general population.* (Peters et al., 1999)

While psychiatrists may concede the point that these types of beliefs are more common than one might first expect, I'm pretty sure they, nevertheless, would probably use the 'irrationality' or 'lack of evidence' card. While not wanting to go down the 'evidence' route of this debate, I can circumnavigate around this issue by saying that spiritual experiences, by definition, usually involve something which cannot be measured by science. The psychiatrist will attempt to use the ruling paradigm to justify their opinion about what you are experiencing, and I feel it will often be a useless task to try to use their paradigm to rationalize your beliefs with them. In addition, you will be adding fuel and weight to their paradigm and hence you will be giving them more power. Especially with this issue when they did not experience what you did. You are the expert here – not them.

Now I'm not saying that they can't provide a useful way of viewing what you have experienced or open up a new avenue to explore it from which could be helpful. Nor am I saying they aren't knowledgeable about their own field – they are, and it certainly has its place. I'm just saying that often the people with power, in these situations, sadly often aren't prepared to view your experience from any other paradigm or approach than the current dominant one. They may be able to help you go through it more calmly or peacefully with or without the use of medication or help you find some safe and supportive place to go to during it.

Let me make it clear right now: I am not; repeat not, anti-psychiatry.

I am merely pointing out its limitations and question its power as a legitimate 'authority' with certain 'mental health conditions'. Some of these limitations become huge, especially when looking at the whole issue of spiritual emergences. It will take a more flexible or more sensitive paradigm to effectively work with and help us who experience these types of spiritual episodes. While some changes seem to be occurring, there is still a lot of work to be done to imbed and make the changes. I feel we need more 'accepted' spiritual forms of practices.

Either way, ultimately you must retain your own power to define what you have been through and therefore ultimately how you shape your own identity. Don't simply let the ruling paradigm, and those with the power, dictate what you think and feel about what you have been through. Science has provided humanity with many great achievements and advances in medicine which have saved lives and healed countless people around the world. When addressing the issue of spiritual emergencies, however, I feel that science is still very limited in its approach to and understanding of these types of experiences. In short, it finds them hard to tolerate as an acceptable difference which doesn't always need suppressing or made to simply disappear.

In summary, we have to help and encourage the education of those with the power and help to heal the 'developed' societal attitude malfunction. Who knows – perhaps one day it might start to generate a new paradigm shift towards one which is more understanding and accepting of our experiences, as common life occurrences, and which get normalized.

I leave you with two final thoughts on this matter. The first is by Rufus May, who is a British psychologist who has experienced a spiritual emergence episode, who concludes his paper with the following:

> *In seeking to help people who speak of alternative realities, our job is to be curious and open-minded. We should not seek to make people*

conform to more dominant beliefs systems in our society. We need to create social spaces where people can share different perspectives and learn new ways of being with others. (May, 2010)

And the second by David Harper, a senior lecturer in clinical psychology, who concludes his paper's abstract by saying:

> *I suggest that we need to be open to service users' own theories of the meaning of their beliefs and see our goal as helping them find better ways of living with them.* (Harper, 2004: 64)

Conclusion: Begin the Healing

I hope that what I have demonstrated in this chapter is that in order to take the power back, we must first understand where the power currently lies, how it got there, and how best to start to re-empower ourselves as well as others in order to correct the current imbalance. This will, I hope, go some way towards helping to heal the 'developed' societal attitude malfunction so that many other people, like me, can live in peace with tolerance and acceptance, and without the fear and anxiety of what stigma and prejudice can cause.

I find it particularly poignant and ironic that it could be us, service-users or patients, who could become the healers in a pretty big way and lead the way forward. Perhaps our 'developed' societies could, one day, truly become developed and enlightened in ways we can only imagine.

I live in hope, and I truly believe that if we all take our rightful power back then we will see this happen. I invite you to join me in making this a reality.

A Thousand Souls Shot

It was the light catching my eye,
An aspect of that which they now have not.
Ghost riders in the sky,
A thousand souls shot.

Men in white coats assigning labels,
Nurses treating the 'rot'.
I'm lying on the table now,
Together with a thousand souls shot.

The liquid drug grips my brain,
With angels I know and now forgot.
I'm alone with spirit traversing this plane,
Along with a thousand souls shot.

The companies' spiritual execution,
The crazies' garrote.
Are they looking for salvation?
So are a thousand souls shot.

I have one mind and vision,
To restore the beautifuls' lot.
Who will speak of a peaceful revolution?
And save all of those who shot.

6

From Break-Down to Break-Through

Awareness is the greatest agent for change.

Eckhart Tolle

When I was in hospital, as described in my first book The Canary: A Journey through Psychosis, I found a crystal one day in the dormitory on the ward. It was a piece of rose quartz, which at the time, held personal significance to me. I held on to that crystal until after leaving hospital I gave it to a friend of mine to leave in a wonderful resting place; the ancient temple ruins of Angkor Wat in Cambodia, as a symbolic gesture of my having come to terms with the ending of a previous love relationship.

I am reminded of that crystal now as I have been, literally, holding on to several crystals more recently. More specifically, since my move to the USA, I remember one stormy and difficult night of fear for me when I knocked one of them (a piece of Aventurine) by mistake onto the stone tiled floor and it broke in two. The two pieces cracked along a natural fissure in the crystal.

That event now holds significance for me as it reminded me, in a very poignant way, several important aspects about what I had been through, and how I then chose to view that 'episode', or what some refer to as being a 'Break-down'.

Firstly, I had viewed the separation of the two pieces as a 'break' of one whole piece. This caused me to get saddened and upset. However, I now realize that if I choose to view it as a 'creation' of two new whole pieces, then I am much happier and also see them for what they truly are.

Secondly, the fissure inside the crystal was always there, ever since its creation no doubt. It was also one of the reasons I had liked it so much as it often caught the light and emitted brilliant rainbow colors. You could say that it was the crystal's 'flaw' if you like that made the crystal so special to me.

People often talk about the nature versus nurture debate in relation to the etiology, or development and manifestation, of mental health 'conditions' or episodes. Most researchers and scientists now believe, however, that for most conditions or episodes, a combination of both nature and nurture (ie. situations, environment, and events in one's life) are significant factors in their occurrence. Just like the crystal, it had its fissure from creation (or from birth,) its 'Nature' if you like – and was knocked on to the floor: 'Nurture' - or life event. It was the combination of the two which caused the 'break'. Therefore, given the right situation in one's life – just like that of the crystal – some of us may potentially 'break' beyond our control if faced with certain life events or situations.

Yet, what does it really mean to 'Break'? And who or what is breaking?

For me at any rate, the only thing I experienced that 'broke-down' were past expectations, assumptions, and opinions about the nature of life and to some extent, about reality itself. Now I'm not saying it wasn't a terrifying experience – nor am I saying my ability to function day to day wasn't impeded – they all were. However, long-term and in hind-sight – the fear and paranoia subsided, and my mind was left intact. In fact, I would add my awareness was also not only intact, but it had also changed for the better; it grew and expanded.

Moreover, my meat-suit and my spirit/soul symbolically speaking, instead of breaking at all – really began to become two separate (and yet interconnected) parts, and my realization of this manifested in my conscious awareness. I do take medication for my meat-suit and brain chemistry; however, I have learnt that my spiritual side co-exists in relationship to what I am physically, and therefore needs as much attention as my body does.

Therefore, nothing truly broke for me. What did occur, however, was a break-through, in thought, being and awareness of a whole new world! To quote the famous Doors song, I literally felt as though I broke "on through to the other side..." – that of the awareness of the world of spirit and of the Self.

I am now also reminded of another song, Leonard Cohen's 'Anthem,' in which he states "There is a crack in everything, that's how the light gets in." In other words, and thirdly, we who have a potential to 'break' might have a strong need for more 'light' on our 'surfaces', or insides so-to-speak. Yet, this increased exposure to self-knowledge, wisdom, creativity, or spiritual awareness can be, however, very difficult to cope with for many who are unprepared or who are unaware of what is occurring for them.

For example, if the opening up to greater amounts of 'light' results in fear, anxiety, and paranoia, then one might argue that the individual is finding it difficult to navigate the waters of awareness to their spiritual nature and being. For as the well-known mythologist Joseph Campbell (1988:13) once said about the difference between the psychological 'crack-up' and the mystic:

> The difference is the one who cracks up is drowning in the water in which the mystic swims.

Two main points are raised within this quote for me. Firstly, both the psychological 'crack- up' and the mystic are both within, or are exploring, the same waters. Secondly, whilst the mystic is able to swim, the person who is 'cracking' is finding it difficult to cope with the 'water' and is being overwhelmed by it all.

That brings us to the inevitable question of what is this 'water'? And how can some swim while others are seemingly drowning? I believe, now, that the 'water' is a symbolic representation of an opening up to – or increased awareness in not only our spiritual side and being but also in a greater awareness of - and interaction with – spirit and the Self.

Having been taught the ways and means of understanding (ie. conceptual 'hooks' and spiritual frameworks) for working with spirit through culture passed down through the generations, the mystic is able to stay at the surface and ride the waves –so-to-speak and go with the 'flow'.

Whereas the individual finding themselves without the necessary understanding, means and methods, for opening up to spirit safely and calmly find themselves quite literally 'drowning' in their own spiritual awareness and often get labeled as being 'Schizophrenic', 'Psychotic' or 'Bipolar' or some other mental health diagnosis. They often are, literally, however, at emergency status spiritually – and thus are undergoing a spiritual emergency.

That being said however, Thomas Szasz (1973: 113) once said (when illustrating the ridiculous view 'modern' westernized society takes when looking at spirit,) that;

> If you talk to God, you are praying; If God talks to you, you have schizophrenia. If the dead talk to you, you are a spiritualist; If you talk to the dead, you are a schizophrenic.

If others believe that of you then that's one thing – but what if YOU believe communication is only a one-way street with God and with spirit for the so-called sane? What if you hear whom you believe to be God's 'voice' or communicate with spirits? Are you automatically mentally unwell? For years I believed this... until one day... I met the community of the Spiritualists Online Network. This community forced me to reflect on many things I thought I 'knew' about myself, the world, and to a large degree about reality itself. In short, they forced me to think on the 'what ifs'; in other words:

What IF I have been really communicating with God and spirit – for real?

However, before I go onto to talk about this and what I've learned to date, I would firstly like to share my system of understanding and a tool for measuring the intensity of any emergence episode with you in the hopes that you may find it a useful aid during your awakening process and help steer you away from any 'drowning' emergencies that may arise.

I Wanna Go Home

I wanna go Home,
To the Home before home...
Where I don't feel distant
From all of you.

I wanna go Home,
To the Home of all homes...
Where the separate outside and inside,
And this existential ache,
Are through.

I wanna go Home,
To the Home that is all there is...
And evolve my awareness
To remembering I am Home,

And that this will always be true.

7

The Divine Balance Approach

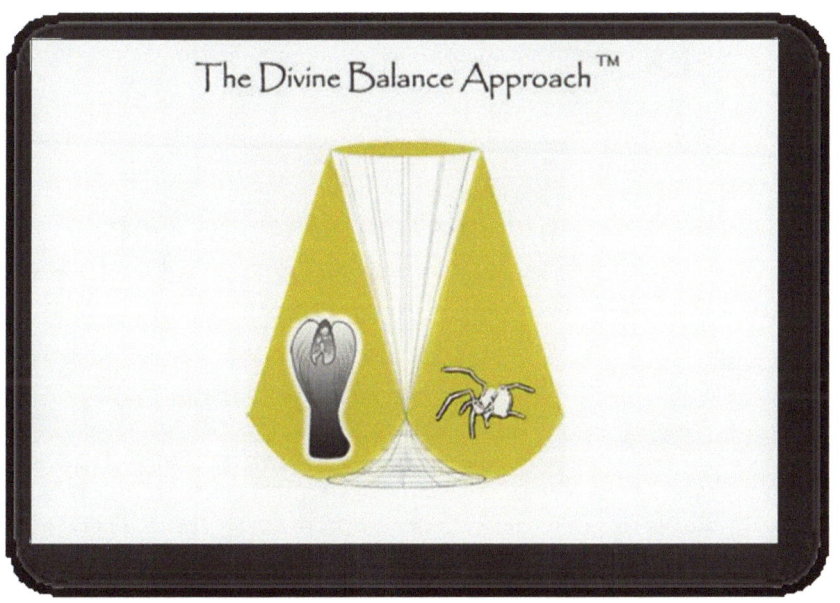

Nature's first green is gold.

Anon

The Divine Balance Approach (or The DBA) is my conceptual framework – or rather my attempt of making sense of what occurred for me during my acute phases of opening up to spirit – my spiritual emergencies – if you like. Whilst the medical establishment would be quick to label my experiences typical of someone exhibiting symptoms of Bipolar Type I Disorder, I have found the following conceptual framework and approach far more pertinent and relevant to the forces at play in my wellbeing – more so than most medical theories.

That being said, what is 'The Divine Balance Approach?' I view it as a unique and deep- rooted yet progressive model of awareness which illustrates several components and forces at play in the process of my increase of spiritual awareness, and knowledge of Self. This process is often called 'spiritual emergence'.

Yet, as we have covered, these types of experiences do not always leave the experiencer in a good place during the episode. Fear, paranoia, anxiety and or deep depression – even psychosis, often can result for some. How can this be so if spirituality is supposed to be uplifting and positive? Well, the 3 forces illustrated in The DBA have, I now believe, been at the core of the formulation, manifestation as well as influenced the outcome of many of my spiritual emergency episodes. The DBA theoretically illustrates how these forces work and how they balance one's emotions throughout the process of the spiritual emergency whether or not one is aware of them.

Let us now take a look at the 3 forces illustrated by The DBA. They are the forces of Ascension, the force of The Dark Angel, and lastly the force of the White Spider. Please note, that these are only metaphors or symbols representing a certain kind of force and are not meant to be taken literally.

Slide 1

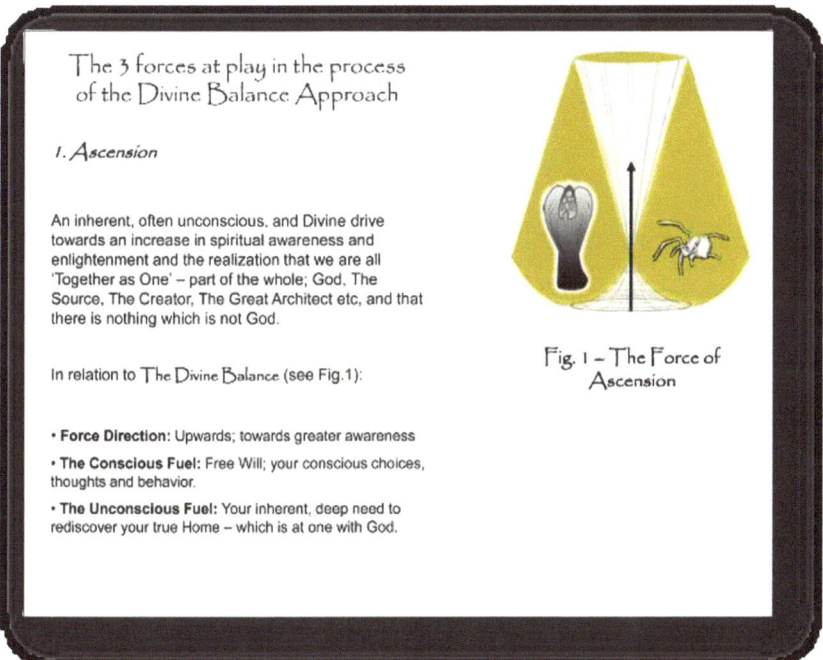

The 3 forces at play in the process of the Divine Balance Approach

1. Ascension

An inherent, often unconscious, and Divine drive towards an increase in spiritual awareness and enlightenment and the realization that we are all 'Together as One' – part of the whole; God, The Source, The Creator, The Great Architect etc, and that there is nothing which is not God.

In relation to The Divine Balance (see Fig.1):

• **Force Direction:** Upwards; towards greater awareness

• **The Conscious Fuel:** Free Will; your conscious choices, thoughts and behavior.

• **The Unconscious Fuel:** Your inherent, deep need to rediscover your true Home – which is at one with God.

Fig. 1 – The Force of Ascension

Let us first look at the force of Ascension. In my experience, Ascension is ...an inherent, often unconscious, and divine drive towards enlightenment and the realization that we are all 'Together as One' – part of the whole; or God, The Source, The Creator, The Great Architect, or Self, and that there is nothing which is not Self.

In Figure 1 on Slide 1, it is represented by the upward arrow – driving one to greater increased spiritual awareness. The fuel, if you like, that governs the magnitude of the force is your own Free Will played out in the choices you make in life from the small ones to the larger ones.

In other words, and according to my life experience to date, I have come to realize that many of the choices I have taken therefore have been governed by this force of Ascension, or the unconscious drive towards an increased spiritual awareness. For I believe that even the tiny choices we make could potentially have big consequences for our development on many levels. Even when we are taking 5 steps forward and two steps back in life, we are still learning and growing: essentially expanding our awareness on many levels – not least on the spiritual level. This is especially true for the mistakes, challenges, and so-called wrong doings in life. Every choice and outcome have a potential for further learning and growth – even the ones that appear not to serve us well.

I now strongly take this view when looking back and reflecting upon my past acute episodes. Despite their being full of fear and terror, and as we will see later in the book, they also offered an opportunity for personal development and growth. Had I not experienced them at all, I wouldn't have had the insight and awareness to make the positive changes in my life and face the fears I needed to evolve spiritually. For today I do believe that *"pain [is] the touchstone of all spiritual progress."* (Alcoholics Anonymous, The Twelve Steps and Twelve Traditions: 93).

Moreover, my difficult life experiences together with my episodes have equipped me – if you will – with some important skills of insight and awareness about the nature of these occurrences so that I'm better able to help support others. Now let's turn our attention to the other two forces.

Slide 2

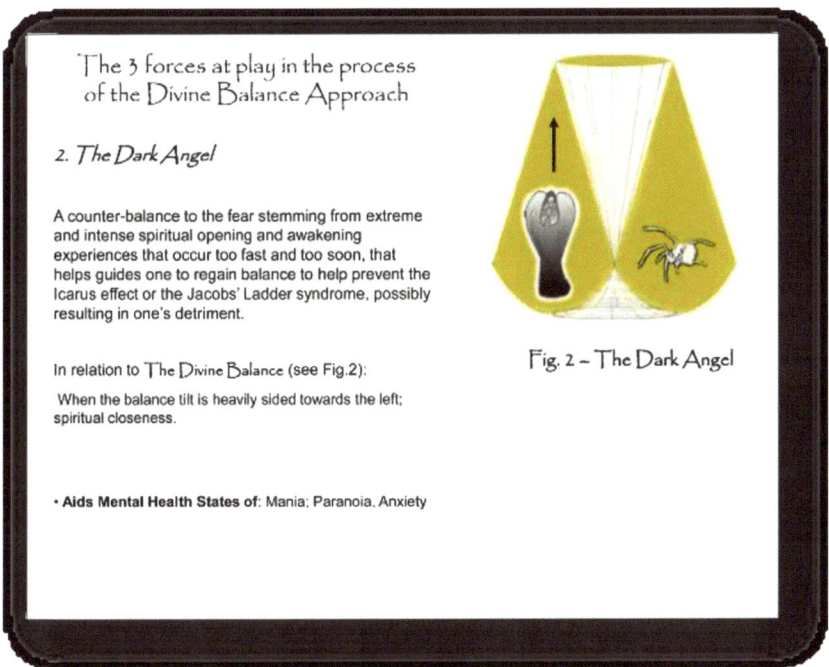

The second force in The DBA is called the force of The Dark Angel. The Dark Angel is a counter-balance force to the fear stemming from projected fear onto God or spirit that guides one to regain balance away from extreme and intense spiritual opening and awakening experiences too fast and too soon. It is a guide to help prevent the Icarus effect or the Jacobs' Ladder syndrome, possibly resulting in one's detriment.

In Figure 2, it is represented on the left weight on the balance helping to re-balance the scale towards the center from the left – driving one to the center's 'middle way path' – more to come on this later.

Slide 3

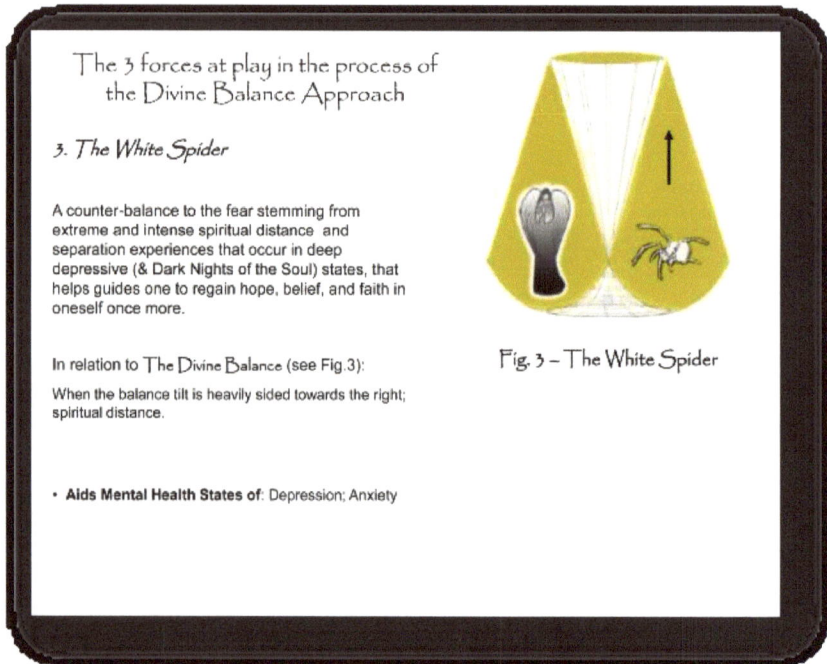

The 3 forces at play in the process of the Divine Balance Approach

3. *The White Spider*

A counter-balance to the fear stemming from extreme and intense spiritual distance and separation experiences that occur in deep depressive (& Dark Nights of the Soul) states, that helps guides one to regain hope, belief, and faith in oneself once more.

In relation to The Divine Balance (see Fig.3):

When the balance tilt is heavily sided towards the right; spiritual distance.

• **Aids Mental Health States of**: Depression; Anxiety

Fig. 3 – The White Spider

The last of the 3 forces in The DBA is called the force of The White Spider. The White Spider is a counter-balance force to the fear stemming from internalized fear onto the Self that guides one to regain balance away from extreme depression, hopelessness and states of despair. It is a guide to help prevent going too far 'inside' oneself and exploring the existential, possibly resulting in one's detriment.

In Figure 3, it is represented on the right weight on the balance helping to re-balance the scale towards the center from the right – driving one inwards towards the 'middle way' path.

Viewed holistically, all three forces work together. The Dark Angel and White Spider forces both push one towards the center's 'middle way' path in life and the force of Ascension pushes one upwards, towards an increase in divine awareness. Now you might ask: "won't people's spiritual development be affected by what religion people believe in? Or what culture people are from? Or spiritual path one follows?"

I would say: Good questions indeed! Now those points are addressed by looking at the Mountain of Awareness in more detail...which is what we are going to do now.

Slide 4

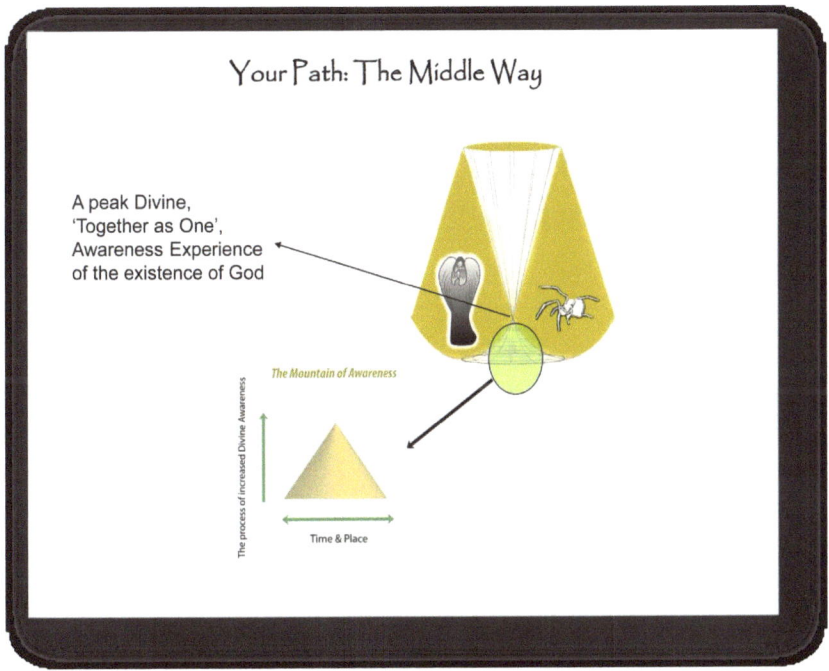

As shown in Slide 4, The Mountain of Awareness is a metaphoric mountain we are all climbing – pushed on by the force of Ascension. It is represented at the base of the Divine Balance of Awareness. Up close – we can see a simplified model of it.

Everyone born in this World is beginning at the base of the mountain. Where exactly is determined by the time and place of their birth. And so they start their ascent. They start their journey either on an established path up the mountain (religion or established spiritual practices) or they may choose to go it alone and forge a new path up the mountain. It simply doesn't matter where you start or how you get there – all paths lead to the same place - the top!

The point is to be aware of the mountain and the 3 forces at work on your spiritual emergence, or awakening journey. It doesn't matter if you believe in God or don't; follow one religion or another – but by simply being aware of these forces in relation to your own spiritual development did I, and so could you, start to make healthier and more harmonious choices in life.

What happens at the top of the mountain?

That is where and when you have your acute awareness moment of the divine nature of everything – that essentially, we are all 'Together as One' – when God/Self touches you and makes Its presence to you known and felt. The classical 'peak' experience. At this point you are acutely aware – from looking up on high – back down the mountain, how all spiritual and/or religious practices and approaches are essentially bringing about the awareness of the same thing: we are One! ...Part of one Whole – part of One God/Self.

The process is then reversed as you must then 'come down from the mountain top' and apply what you have learnt in everyday life. In the diagram – this is the long and inverted mountain shape above The Mountain of Awareness's peak. It is situated above the peak experience as the force of Ascension is still very much at play in your awareness and development as you further expand and mature spiritually.

Slide 5

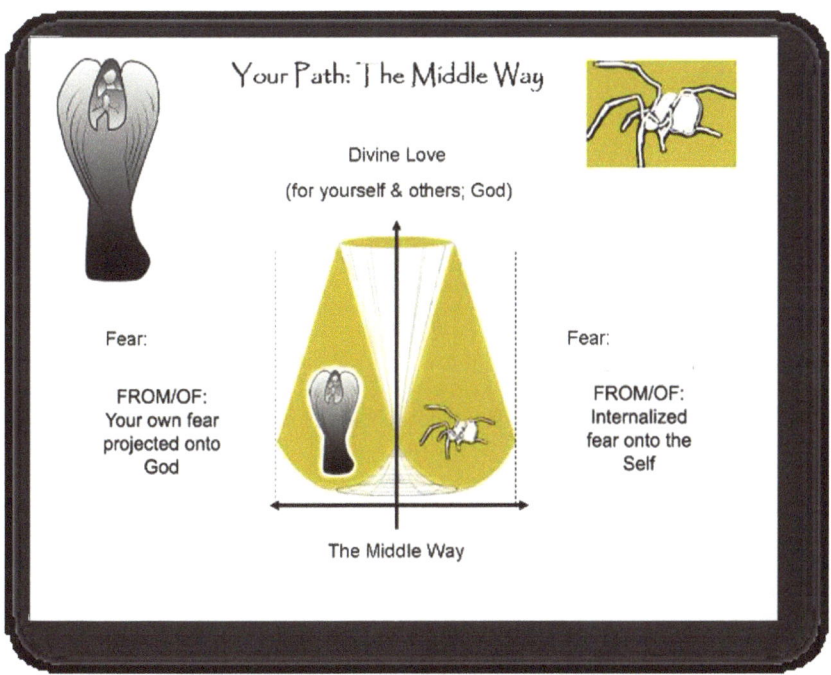

What about love? Where does it fit in?

Well, there are only two primary emotions in life = love and fear. Fear results in a whole host of other symptoms (masking emotions) = like hostility, anger, sadness, guilt, anxiety etc.

Now some might say – in relation to this approach – that fear results from extreme judgment – from either a belief in an external God source and your beliefs about His judgment of you, or from your own judgment beliefs about yourself.

However, as we all employ and 'filter' experiences about ourselves and the world around us using our mental 'filters' of past experiences, values and beliefs, and so on, it becomes apparent that the only true source of fear is oneself.

As one becomes 'closer' to God/Self (or the awareness of Her presence), one also, and naturally I would add, becomes acutely aware of one's own 'sins', misdeeds, or wrong doings in life – however one might define them. This heightens tension and anxiety in oneself to a point that one is left either internalizing the fear and anxiety inwards – with the Self being the primary object of fear; or projecting it outwards, with God Herself (or spirit) as well as other people being the object of fear.

Love (and therefore positive spiritual emergence experiences) results from becoming aware of and maintaining: Your healthy average 'middle way path' – ie, the divine balance between to the two extremes of fear, I now believe.

Love is the total absence of fear, or more specifically the effects of fear – from either side which can be found by finding your own middle way path – your own unique balance – as you progress up the mountain.

Do be mindful, however, that as one progresses with life's journey of spiritual awareness that this balance, or average, WILL change over time (as you become more spiritually aware) and is also unique to YOU. There are no right or wrong averages – no 'ideal' middle way paths to take that can be generalized for all to follow.

The middle way ascension line drawn here is only in the center of the two forces of the Dark Angel and the White Spider for illustrative purposes only. Your healthy middle way average may be closer to the Dark Angel side or to the White Spider's. What is one person's health middle way path and balance may be unhealthy for another.

The Divine Balance Approach is not, therefore, a religion or a spiritual discipline to practice and adhere to. It is simply a framework - you take from it what you will and do with it what you will. The choice, as ever, is up to YOU! ...Always has been and always will be! That's free Will.

The key is INSIGHT and AWARENESS into the 3 forces at play in your life and spiritual awareness (or emergence and awakening) process.

How do I gain insight and awareness into the forces at play in my life?

...By using the Spiritual Emergence Intensity Tool (or THE SEIT.)

8

~~~

The Spiritual Emergence
Intensity Tool

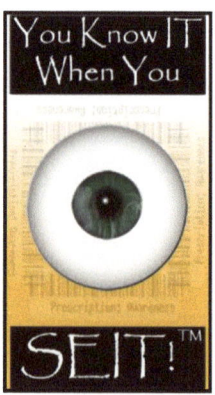

When I see I am nothing, that is wisdom.
When I see I am everything, that is love.
And between these two,
My life flows.

Nisargadatta Maharaj

Now that you have gained some insight into the underlining principles and forces I believe were at play during all of my episodes, it is my hope that you will find the following, one-of-a-kind, spiritual emergence measuring and guidance tool; The Spiritual Emergence Intensity Tool (The SEIT,) useful in measuring the two primary counter-balances at play in your episodes or difficult life challenges towards helping you re-establishing a healthy 'middle-way' balance.

What is The SEIT?

The SEIT is essentially a self-rating tool designed to be your companion during your spiritual awakening journey, through both the good as well as the challenging times.

Whilst often uplifting, powerful, and profound, the spiritual emergence process can also sometimes become difficult to navigate. The SEIT will be an ally; it will promote insight, stability, recovery, as well as foster a real sense of empowerment before, during and after the awakening process.

In short, it will help you to quantify the strength or influence of both The Dark Angel and The White Spider counterbalances in your life in any one day, over time. As such, its uses are many and are unique to each of you. Use it how you want to, but the following is my approach to using it, as well as what to do with the results produced.

The SEIT Design Overview

The SEIT is made up of two self-rating tools, or 'awareness wheels' each with ten emotions at the tip of their ten spokes. The user rates how they feel out of 0-10, using the radio buttons for emotion category. Only one rating can be chosen for each emotion. As far as what the emotion means, it's based on your definition, so keep the meaning consistent every time you use The SEIT.

Figure 1 - The SEIT Closeness Wheel

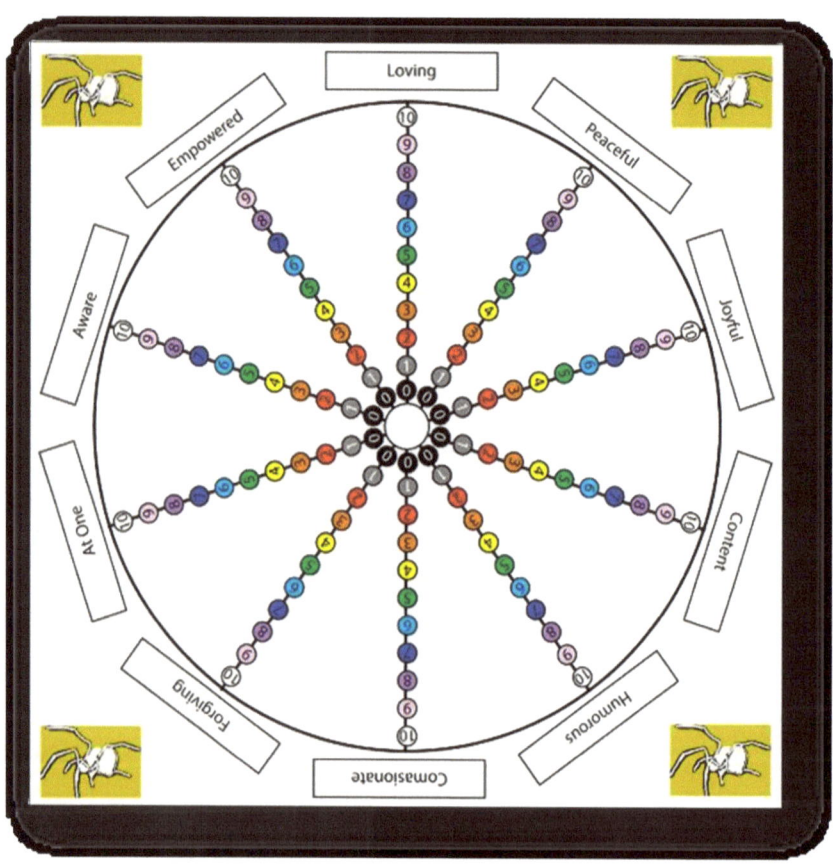

Figure 2 - The SEIT Distance Wheel

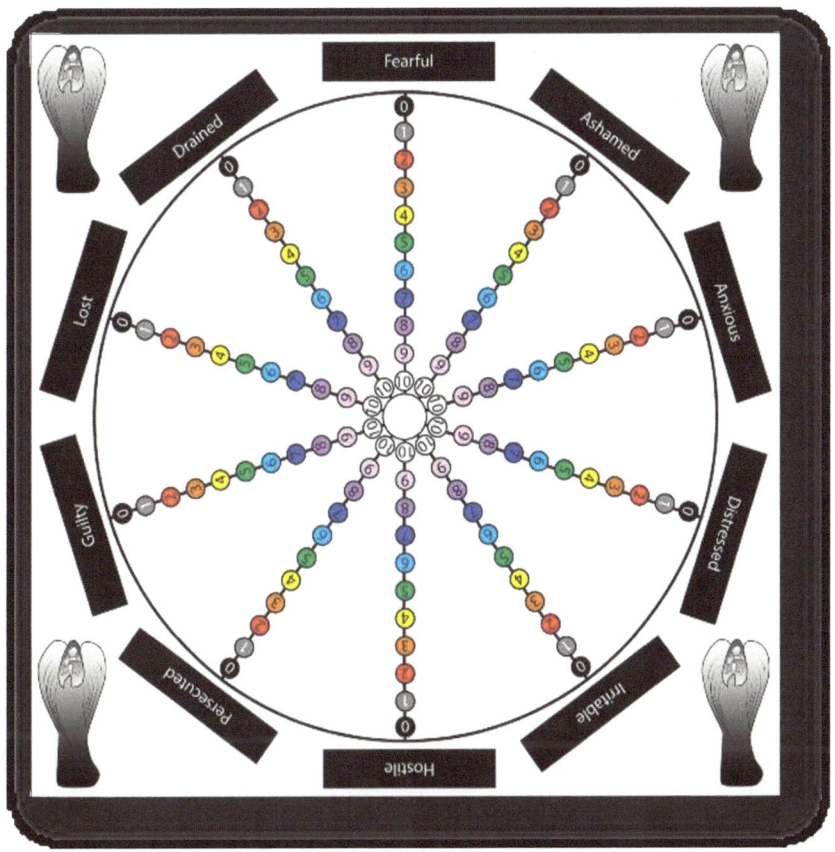

Both Wheels are Copyleft, free to photocopy or scan for personal use only. For all other uses, please contact the author at bio.site/jeffmalderez for permission.

The force of both the dark angel and white spider are towards the edges of each respective wheel. Whilst both the dark angel and the white spider are your allies during your emergence process, they differ in that the white spider nudges one out of the depressive (or deep rest) state, and the dark angel cautions you from opening up too much, too fast. Essentially, they are symbolic representations of the forces at play during a spiritual emergence episode helping one to find their own middle ground – or middle way path – up the mountain of awareness during spiritual ascension.

The Data Organization & Calculations

After one has completed both sets of distance wheels each day for a period of time (I normally do it after a month's time,) it's time to analyze the data. For each distance wheel, one simply counts up the radio buttons' number value for a score for that particular wheel out of 100 (10 number values for each wheel.) The resulting total number is the percent that that particular force (Dark Angel or White Spider) was putting on you on that given day.

Now instead of plotting each separate wheel's data on a X-Y line graph separately, I like to combine both wheels' percent scores on one graph – with a twist. Instead of going from left to right (as in the case of a typical line graph,) my graph starts from the bottom and goes up with the days in the month, together with the corresponding percent totals for each wheel along the now horizontal line (similar to our Mountain of Awareness discussed earlier.)

After plotting several weeks' worth of data, an example graph would look like the graph in Figure 3.

Figure 3 - The SEIT Daily Output Graph

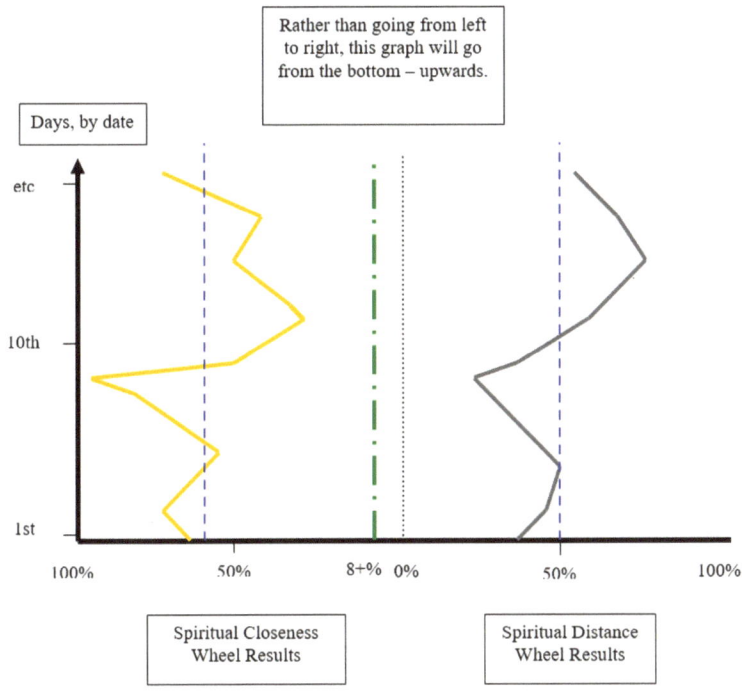

— — — — — · Represents the mean (average) percentage of all the recorded scores to date for both the closeness star and the distance star respectfully.

— · — · — Represents the average 'swing' of both averages in relation to the graph where 0% is centered.

Whilst the above set of data is purely illustrative and made-up, I hope that those of you who like to see visual representations of the forces at play in their life will get some idea of how to apply their data visually. Once you have gained insight as to how and to what degree each force is impacting on you day-by-day, you can then take steps to change the balance if need be – or maintain it if you are feeling good.

For I firmly believe, spiritual 'sanity' can be described in part by saying it is the ability to control the intensity of spiritual awareness and signs, as well as your focus on them, whilst maintaining faith in hope, and insight throughout the episode.

How does one do that? Well, it is my hope that Part Two, coming up, will guide you through some of the steps I take.

Part Two: From Spiritual Emergence to Awareness of Self

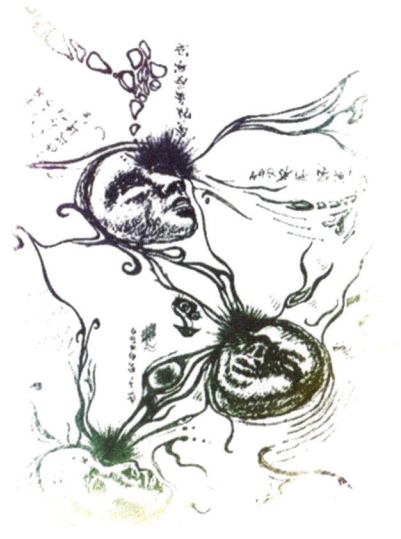

"Knowing" God means "Being" God, it is not relative knowledge.

Ramana Maharshi

A Koan: A Student of Being

I am a student of being.
Or, I have been,
For now I am awakening.

To play or not to play,
To hide or seek,
Were the questions,
Dancing around the eternal circle of life's choice of awareness.

Reality fossilized in thought by consciousness,
Was the foolish game,
I once was playing with myself:

"Start stopping...Stop starting..."

Now, in this moment,
I live free,
Outside the pressure box:
To be...

...A Student of Being

I am a student of being.
Or, I have been,
For now I am awakening.

To play or not to play,
To hide or seek,
Were the questions,
Dancing around the eternal circle of life's choice of awareness.
Reality fossilized in thought by consciousness,
Was the foolish game,
I once was playing with myself:

"Start stopping...Stop starting..."

Now, in this moment,
I live free,
Outside the pressure box:

To be...

9

Personal Development

If your compassion does not include yourself, then it is incomplete.

Buddha

Journey to the Self: An Adventure in Spiritual Development

Welcome, dear reader, to the next leg of our journey—a journey of personal development. In this chapter, we will explore the twists, turns, and delightful pitfalls of personal growth through the lens of Advaita Vedanta, the tradition of non-duality. I have chosen this viewpoint and model, and practice, to unpack for it most closely aligns with my life's spiritual episodes and experiences to date. Buckle up, keep your sense of humor close, and prepare for some profound (and perhaps some humorous) insights.

The Cosmic Comedy of Self-Improvement

Let's face it: personal development can sometimes feel like an elaborate cosmic joke. Just when you think you've "got it all together," life has a way of throwing you a curveball, reminding you that the journey is never truly over. And isn't that beautiful? The universe keeps us on our toes, dancing to the rhythm of self-discovery.

In the spirit of Advaita Vedanta, we start with the premise that at the deepest level, we are already whole and complete. Our true Self is like a brilliant diamond, covered in the muck of life's experiences and ego-driven drama. Personal development is less about becoming someone new and more about uncovering the radiant being we already are.

Embracing the Divine Messiness

One of the core teachings of Advaita Vedanta is that the Self is not separate from the universe. Everything you experience—the joys, the sorrows, the triumphs, and the failures—are all expressions of the same divine play (Lila). So, when you trip over your own feet on the path of self-improvement, remember it's all part of the cosmic dance.

Imagine you're at a grand masquerade ball. At first, you're caught up in the excitement, the costumes, and the characters. But as the night progresses, you start to see through the masks. Personal development is like that—peeling away the layers of false identity until you recognize the divine in yourself and others.

The Art of Self-Love

Now, let's talk about love—universal love, to be precise. Advaita Vedanta teaches that love is our natural state, the glue that holds the cosmos together. But here's the kicker: you can't truly love others until you love yourself. Yes, it's that classic airline safety advice—secure your own oxygen mask before helping others.

Self-love isn't about narcissism; it's about recognizing your intrinsic worth. It's about being gentle with yourself, forgiving your mistakes, and celebrating your progress. It's about standing in front of the mirror, looking deep into your own eyes, and saying, "I am enough and necessary – by virtue of being at all."

Practicing Presence

One of the greatest gifts you can give yourself is the practice of presence. In the hustle and bustle of modern life, it's easy to get lost in the noise. But true personal development happens in the quiet moments of stillness.

Picture this: you're sitting in your favorite chair, a cup of coffee in hand, watching the sunrise. For a moment, the mind chatter stops, and you simply are. In these moments, you touch the essence of your being —pure, unbounded awareness.

The Power of Humor

And finally, let's not forget the power of humor. Spiritual development doesn't have to be all serious and somber. Laugh at the absurdity of it all! After all, if the universe is a grand play, then why not enjoy it?

Next time you catch yourself taking life too seriously, remember the wise words of the mystic Rumi: "Sell your cleverness and buy bewilderment." Embrace the mystery, laugh at the folly, and dance your way through this adventure called life.

Conclusion: Homecoming

As we journey through personal development, we are not so much changing as we are returning—coming home to our true Self. David Bowie once commented that: "Aging is an extraordinary process whereby you become the person you always should have been." This path of the Self is both profound and playful, a sacred adventure filled with love, laughter, and light.

So, dear traveler, keep your heart open, your spirit light, and your sense of humor intact. Remember that you are already whole, already divine, and every step you take is a step closer to remembering that truth. Together, let us embrace the cosmic dance, with all its glorious messiness, and celebrate the magnificent, radiant beings that we are.

Welcome home.

The Key

These are the words that I hold true,
These are the words that I give to you.

These are the words I believe,
And I hope that you will too.

I do more, and yet it's always less...
I understand much, and yet it's nothing best...

I feel the World, and it's hard to bear.
Do I understand? no....

But I do care...

I don't want praise, for I know my own self- worth.
I don't want rewards; for I whisper "it is within rebirth."

I don't have the key, and yet I want to give that to you...
To unlock love's cage, and witness your soul anew.

❧⦿❧

10

Spiritual Integrity

Doubt is the veil that blocks our awareness of Self.

Jeff Malderez

When I was living and working back in England for the National Health Services' Mental Health Trust, I used to be responsible for facilitating a variety of group sessions for people engaged with services. One of these groups was called Relaxation, and I often used to take people on a guided relaxation rich in visual imagery.

My favorite session I liked to do was one I had developed from my own visual meditations called The Stream. After some progressive muscle relaxation techniques and some deep breathing, I would guide the participants through a meadow of wildflowers down towards a row of trees. On the other side of the trees, I described a stream in front of the participants where a blanket was laying on the ground underneath a big oak tree on the bankside of the stream. After inviting the participants to sit down on the blanket and make themselves comfortable, I would then draw their attention towards the surface of the stream.

Upon the surface of the stream, I would describe a variety of leaves, twigs and small branches being washed downstream passing right in front of them as they watched. I then told the participants that each piece of debris being washed down stream was a single thought or idea that the participant was experiencing at that moment in their own 'stream' of consciousness. After giving time to observe and assign thoughts and ideas to each leaf, twig or small branch, I would then describe a process of acknowledging, embracing or accepting, and releasing or 'letting go.'

The first step in this process was to 'acknowledge', or become aware, of what one was thinking. Out of the corner of their mind's eye, I invited participants to simply observe all the thoughts and ideas or even images they were experiencing in each passing moment – whilst at the same time not trying to stop any of them, rather simply letting them all 'bubble up' to the surface and 'flow' into view or awareness.

The second step was then described. This step is the part of the process in which one is asked to 'embrace' or 'accept' the fact they are experiencing those thoughts, ideas or images, be they positive or negative, without any judgment as to what the thoughts were about or if they were positive thoughts or not.

Lastly, the third step was described for the participants; the step of 'releasing' or 'letting go' of every thought or idea they witnessed passing past their conscious awareness, just like an objective observer might do. Instead of wading into the stream and holding on to each twig, small branch, or thought/idea, and letting it carry one down the stream, I asked for participants to focus their attention back into the current moment's next thought or idea.

Whilst some found it easier to do than others, those that did manage to keep the process going during their relaxation session reported feeling more calm and peaceful by and large than those who found it difficult to achieve. I then often invited participants to discuss their session with others and to share any thoughts they found hard not to either embrace or accept without judgment, or ideas or thoughts that were difficult to let go or release. We often then discussed some of the possible causes for these challenges that went some way towards their recovery at large.

I am reminded, now, of these relaxation sessions for when I started taking a class on Spiritual Integrity created and taught by an online spiritual community. I was amazed how close the processes of Spiritual Integrity and my relaxation session, The Stream, were.

During many weeks of meeting with the instructor and my fellow classmates, my personal development was to take a turn deeper than ever before.

What I discovered was that in taking a closer look at my own spiritual integrity, I am now better able to free up many blockages and challenges that were essentially holding me back in so many ways and clear a lot of the doubt of who and what I really am; that is to say a spiritual being of light who loves to help others using my own personal experience and abilities, who adores being creative and sharing these with friends and family.

So, what in fact is Spiritual Integrity you might ask? Well, Spiritual Integrity is the internal walk that one takes on their own spiritual journey. In other words, it's knowing 'you' from the inside-out and accepting that part of you. Like with The Stream, the process of Spiritual Integrity has three parts to it; Mental Integrity; Emotional Integrity; and Physical Integrity.

Mental Integrity can be defined as being the 'chitter-chatter' in one's head that can be both positive and negative. In other words, it is what you think and why you think it. Sadly, and all too often, these thoughts can be unkind and not always loving towards oneself.

These negative thought patterns often have at their core, or root, a past event or 'trigger' which formed the basis for their creation, often during childhood, as a learned maladaptive response which persists to the current day. An example of such a thought pattern might be that one believes they are a 'weirdo' or 'freak' and repeatedly tell themselves this in their head which leads to low self-esteem, feelings of being misunderstood or of being an outsider, and perhaps also of being unloved or accepted by others.

Emotional Integrity can be defined as being how one emotionally reacts towards life's challenges. In other words, you could also say, it is how Mental Integrity and outside influences (people, situations, or events) affect one emotionally. Following on from the example above, an example of Emotional Integrity might be to feel the emotions of sadness, worthlessness (if turned inwards) and possibly anger or even hatred for others (if turned outwards,) following on from, and in response to, the negative thought pattern of believing oneself to be a 'weirdo' or 'freak'.

Physical Integrity can be defined as being the choices one makes during one's own spiritual walk in life. In other words, it is the 'follow-through' from Emotional Integrity, or how we all act in response to our emotional state in any given moment or situation.

Following, again, on from the example above, an example of Physical Integrity might be that the individual believing themselves to be a 'weirdo/freak,' and who experiences the inward-focused emotions of sadness and worthlessness, might then choose to act accordingly by withdrawing away from society at large and might also not engage in conversation with others. Should they experience the latter emotions of hatred or anger, they might be verbally aggressive in pitch and tone of voice towards others and say things they might later regret.

So, how can Spiritual Integrity be developed positively speaking? Well, as with many things in life, we have at our disposal three main tools. These are Discernment, Love, and Forgiveness. These tools are used in conjunction with the three steps within each category of Spiritual Integrity that one decides to follow in order to grow and mature along one's own spiritual path. These three steps are:

Step 1) Acknowledge
Step 2) Embrace
Step 3) Release

Put simply, the first step of Acknowledgement is to accept and 'own' what you own – that which is yours. Using discernment here to ascertain that which is yours and that which is others', is an important step of 'knowing thy Self.' The next step of Embracing, is to go some way towards 'loving thy Self,' and to ask why am I experiencing these thoughts, emotions, or doing and saying these things? If these are negative, embrace them regardless, but understand where they are coming from, for they still make you – YOU, and hold valuable lessons to learn from. Lastly, the third step is to Release. This process of 'letting go' most often calls for the tool of forgiveness towards yourself (and others.)

In summary, if all three tools are used together with each three categories of Spiritual Integrity within each of the three steps, then it is my opinion that the individual will become a more mindful; more balanced; and more spiritually aware person as a result.

This is supported by many of the great religious texts known today as well as in the inscriptions at Luxor, by the ancient Egyptians, which are probably the earliest record of the proverb "*Know thy self, for the Kingdom of God is within us.*"

To my mind and heart, for one to become aware of this experientially, or in everyday life experiences, then one must address one's internal walk of self. Because to know self, before others, builds love and learning in an internal way, that we carry with us forward along our own spiritual journey. For if one truly knows what it is to 'Know thy Self,' 'Love thy Self,' and 'Forgive thy Self' then the doorways for greater awareness of spirit and the universal connection that we all share become available in a way I suspect I can only begin to imagine – but am beginning to learn.

So, I invite you to look at your own spiritual integrity and see how it all fits in with you and your spiritual walk in life as well as with your own spiritual development. The following two tables might help you in ascertaining how best to make use of discernment, love, and forgiveness in your own spiritual walk to better your own growth and development. The first table will summarize the 'what' of Spiritual Integrity with explanations for each three parts, and for each of the three steps respectively. The second table is for you to use, to aid you in your own spiritual integrity process with patterns of thought or triggers which seem to be holding you back or that you want to work on.

Some things you might want to explore and look at are the root triggers for the following emotions/actions (and then their resulting Physical choices) as a result:

- Comparing
- Competing
- Judgments
- Anger
- Regrets
- Worry
- Blame
- Guilt
- Hate
- Fear

Table 1 - The 'What' of Spiritual Integrity

Spiritual Integrity: *The internal walk one takes on their own spiritual journey*	Step 1 'Acknowledge' *Know thy Self*	Step 2 'Embrace' *Love thy Self*	Step 3 'Release' *Forgive thy Self*
Mental Integrity: *The chitter-chatter in one's head which can be both negative and positive*	Having an awareness of your thought patterns, and owning them, is the first step in acknowledging and discerning what is yours and what is others'. The negative patterns are most often responsible for blockages in one's spiritual walk and further awareness.	Asking why you are having the thoughts is crucial here. Embracing your own 'chatter' and facing it head-on is the next step. Often your past will be responsible for its development and need to be re-addressed to see if they are valid thoughts or not.	Forgiving yourself and others is important for the final step of releasing negative thought patterns. Unresolved patterns will come back if the lessons are not learned, and unconditional love not applied.
Emotional Integrity: *How one emotionally reacts towards life challenges*	Bringing awareness to how one feels or emotionally reacts to the above thoughts is the next stage. Are they your	Embracing your emotions, be they positive or negative, is an important next step. Asking why they are there, and getting to the past	'Letting go' of negative emotions is the next step. Once you become aware of how your thoughts affect your feelings, and unconditional love

	emotions or are you being projected upon by others? If they are yours, however, own them.	situational 'trigger', will aid the embracing process.	and forgiveness is applied, it becomes easier to accomplish.
Physical Integrity: *The choices one makes during one's own walk*	The resulting choices of speech and behavior following our emotions now need to be examined. Are they always in your and others' best interests? We all ultimately decide how to re-act to certain emotions and situations. Own that fact.	Embracing the <u>fact</u> we have a choice, and sometimes act not in our own best interest offers us a learning opportunity for spiritual growth. Why did I act that way? Facing these tough questions lead more smoothly to their 'release' and future spiritual growth.	Lastly, the role of truly loving and forgiving oneself and others in tough situations and past events becomes central now. Lessons repeat until learned, but there is no race. We all learn to 'release,' 'let go,' and develop at our own chosen rate.

Table 2 – Your Spiritual Integrity

Spiritual Integrity: *The internal walk one takes on their own spiritual journey*	Step 1 'Acknowledge' *Know thy Self*	Step 2 'Embrace' *Love thy Self*	Step 3 'Release' *Forgive thy Self*
Mental Integrity: *The chitter-chatter in one's head which can be both negative and positive*			
Emotional Integrity: *How one emotionally reacts towards life challenges*			
Physical Integrity: *The choices one makes during one's own walk*			

11

〰️

The Signal

A Cathartic Challenge

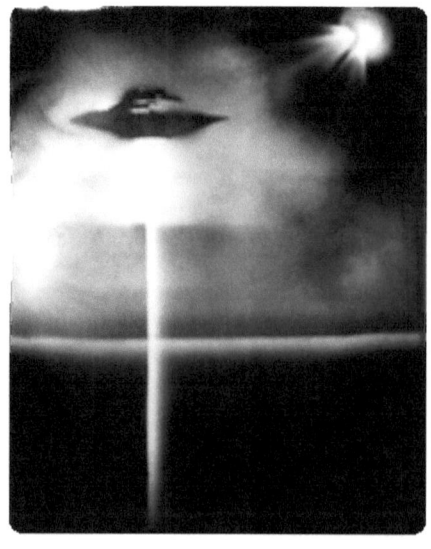

The closer you are to the light, the darker the shadow.

Plato

As Morcheeba sings in their song 'Fear and Love';

> *"We always have a choice, or at least I think we do. We can always use our voice. I thought this to be true. We can live in fear – or extend ourselves to love. We can fall below or lift ourselves above. Fear can stop you loving. Love can stop your fear. Fear can stop you loving. But it's not always that clear."*

Perhaps the deepest and darkest of all challenges to face head on is that of fear. Well it is for me. Yet, by making the conscious choice to face one's fear – re-live it if need be, re- experience the emotions, thoughts and ideas once again, forces the self to make a choice: either be ruled still by terror of the contents of one's 'shadow' – that is to say that which is cast into darkness of the sub-conscious by the light of consciousness – or make a choice that fear does not control you.

By my sharing and writing this fear of mine here and now, I am making this choice; to say to my fears: "You have no power over me."

So what was one of my fears? Since The Canary: A Journey through Psychosis and before, I had long been fascinated by UFOs and aliens. For a few years I was a member of BUFORA – or The British UFO Research Organization and met many well-known people in the field of Ufology. I was convinced aliens or EBEs (Extra-terrestrial Biological Entities) existed and have visited Earth in UFOs.

I still, to this day, believe they exist. However, my old fear was not the fact that they do indeed exist, but rather lies in their motives – or their intent. For this reason, I wish to not focus my debate here on whether they exist, but instead on the old primary fear of my own involvement in the EBEs' mission.

Since the chapter 'Can I have a Light?" in The Canary, and since several spiritual emergency episodes later, I have come to realize my deepest and darkest fear. That I play the pawn in the galactic struggle – which I believed – could end everything: Earth, Humanity, the Sun, The Universe and even the divine.

My theory was that those individuals who have partaken of illicit substances could have 'unlocked' or opened the gateway for EBEs to gain control of their mind and thoughts.

Having done so, the EBEs then gain access to all the person's knowledge and thoughts and uses that to 'navigate' towards the secrets of humanity and the 'location', or essence, of the divine – all with a view to destroy it. In The Canary – I was the EBE's 'mind- controlled' pawn, it strongly felt like, and they were using me and my mind to gain knowledge to target our Sun. Once obtained – they would then destroy it – and with it, all of Humanity. Having believed this, I was prepared to do anything to prevent this from happening – including ending my life.

Since the time of The Canary, this fear-theory of mine escalated to the point where the EBEs subsequently try to obtain control and access to all Humanity's knowledge and information via the internet and other electronic devices. This all came to a head when a good friend of mine sent me the DVD of the movie called The Signal. It 'triggered' me in a big way... I stopped watching it halfway through thinking "oh my God!" how could the writer know of my experiences?! This must surely be validation for and of my theories and experience! I then went into panic mode...

I had sunk into a PTSD-like state, re-living my experiences from The Canary and subsequent times. And yet, my thoughts kept coming back to not only were my experiences of EBE-interference all true but that I wasn't alone! Others were involved...

When I stopped watching the movie and spoke to Jody Morrison – my good friend and spiritual mentor – was it that I realized I had not only been sent the movie for a very positive reason and challenge – but that it was also going to help set me free from some of my fears.

In short, I needed to separate possible reality and truth from fear. All too often people get paranoid and obsessed with the Truth, without acknowledging what emotions that might bring them. The drive for Truth is a hard quest to ignore, but if it doesn't serve your best interest – then ignore it one must. That is exactly what I'm doing now. Not that it isn't important, only that it doesn't serve me well nor could I convince the World they exist.

So, what am I left with? A process of challenging a fear – a cathartic test if you will - and for this I must get to the root of the issue, no matter how scary it might be. Let us now employ the process of spiritual integrity going forward...

Table 3 - The Signal: My Cathartic Challenge of Spiritual Integrity

Spiritual Integrity: *The internal walk one takes on their own spiritual journey*	Step 1 'Acknowledge' *Know thy Self*	Step 2 'Embrace' *Love thy Self*	Step 3 'Release' *Forgive thy Self*
Mental Integrity: *The chitter-chatter in one's head which can be both negative and positive*	I now know that I think and believe that EBEs are controlling me and my thoughts for their malevolent intent. Moreover, that I invest certain energy in them to prove 'their' existence.	Having learned a great deal of evidence of their existence, it's little wonder that I believe they exist. That being said, and regardless, I allow my thoughts to believe; with fear or not.	I 'know' now that this is a pattern of mine – a mental 'habit of mind'. And yet, there ARE other choices I can 'feel' and believe. That being said – I forgive myself for feeling what I have thought and felt.
Emotional Integrity: *How one emotionally reacts towards life challenges*	These thoughts and beliefs create fear and paranoia in me, as well as terror.	If your thoughts and theories are indeed true, then no wonder you are scared and full of fear. I allow you to feel them and know that you loved.	Knowing that I did and would do my best to halt their malevolent intentions, I choose to feel content regardless of my thoughts. The 'facts' and my feelings are not mutually inclusive.
Physical Integrity:	I talk in terms of trying to stop or halt the EBE's actions and so my	And yet, I still have a choice; either be ruled by fear about a 'what	I now have come full circle, and CHOOSE to forgive and release

| The choices one makes during one's own walk | behavior is often scared, skittish, and I try to 'control' or blank out my thoughts and speech. | if or choose the opposite; 'what if not'. | myself and the EBEs in love and forgiveness. And give unconditional love to them and myself so my fears dissolve. |

I wish to end this chapter with a piece I was recently 'given':

"In solitude and in rest, know that we are all working for your best.
In spirit and with soul, you walk your path... not knowing the rest... and that is all ok.
Stop and breathe.
"For when one is in-tune with the unknown, the known becomes peaceful"
we whisper into your heart.
Release all fears and all tears... for you will be cleansed and healed.

Aché."

To Whom It May Concern

By Jody Morrison

To Who It May Concern
This note is for you.
Yes! YOU....

Did you think we weren't listening?
That you cried out to us and We did not hear?
Did you think that because Your answers were not loud And clear
And immediate
That we had deserted you?

What part of the do-it-yourself movement did you not get?

We adore you.
You know that; And so
You think that when you ask, you should Receive.
And... Oh yes!

You most certainly do Receive
But
It is not always in the form you hunger for.

Some times
Our greatest gift to you is time
and the tasting of your own Wisdom
And the taking of your own steps, Your own way, so
You can learn and grow and move.
And feel your own power,

Not always
Relying on ours.

Sometimes the loudest response we can give you is silence.

12

Empathy

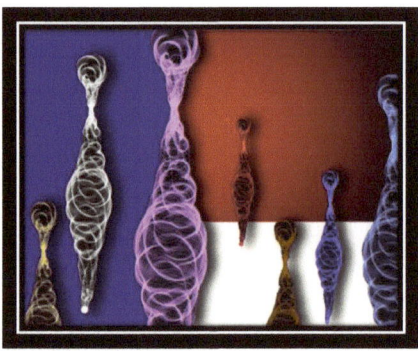

Empathy is about finding echoes of another person in yourself.

Mohsin Hamid

Empathy: The Art of Feeling Together

Welcome, intrepid reader, to another chapter of our spiritual odyssey. We've journeyed through personal development, laughed at the cosmic joke, and embraced our true selves. Now, let's dive into a practice that binds us all together—empathy. Grab a comfy seat, perhaps another cup of coffee, and let's explore the heart of empathy through the lens of Advaita Vedanta, a model of existence that I now strongly connect with, and which informs my actions and ideas about life and the Self.

The Empathic Connection

Empathy, in its essence, is about feeling with others. It's the magical ability to step into someone else's shoes, to share their joy, their pain, and their journey. In the tradition of Advaita Vedanta, this isn't just a nice-to-have skill; it's a recognition of our inherent oneness.

Imagine the universe as a grand symphony, each of us playing our unique instrument.

Empathy is the music that arises when we listen to each other's notes, blending into a harmonious whole. When you tune into someone else's experience, you're not just hearing their song; you're resonating with it, creating a beautiful duet of shared understanding.

The Divine Mirror

In the realm of non-duality, there's no separation between "me" and "you." We are reflections of each other, like myriad facets of the same diamond. When you feel empathy, you're essentially recognizing yourself in the other person. It's like looking into a mirror and seeing a familiar face, but with different stories and experiences etched into the lines.

Think of it this way: if life were a grand masquerade ball (yes, we're back to the ball metaphor—it's a good one!), empathy would be the moment when you realize that beneath all the masks and costumes, everyone is dancing to the same rhythm. You see their struggles, their triumphs, and you realize that they're echoes of your own.

The Power of Presence

To truly empathize, you must be present. Empathy isn't something you can do on the fly while checking your phone or thinking about dinner. It requires your full attention, your heart's engagement.

Picture yourself sitting with a friend who's sharing their troubles. You listen intently, not just with your ears but with your whole being. You're not thinking about what to say next or how to fix their problem; you're simply there, fully present. In those moments, your presence becomes a gift, a silent affirmation that they're not alone.

The Dance of Emotions

Empathy involves a delicate dance with emotions. It's about feeling another's sorrow without drowning in it, sharing their joy without clinging to it. It's like surfing—you ride the emotional waves without getting swept away.

Remember, empathy doesn't mean taking on someone else's emotional baggage.

You're a compassionate surfer, not a sponge. When you feel another's pain, you acknowledge it, sit with it, but you don't let it weigh you down. You offer your support, your understanding, and then gently release it, maintaining your own balance.

Humor: The Empath's Ally

A touch of humor can be a wonderful ally in empathy. It doesn't mean making light of someone's struggles, but rather, finding those moments of lightness that remind us of our shared humanity. Laughter can bridge gaps, dissolve barriers, and create a sense of camaraderie.

When your friend is feeling down, a well-timed, gentle joke can lift their spirits. It's like a wink from the universe, saying, "We're in this together." Humor, when used with sensitivity, can transform a moment of despair into one of connection and hope.

Cultivating Empathy

Cultivating empathy is like tending a garden. It requires patience, attention, and care.

Here are a few practices to nurture your empathic abilities:

1. Active Listening: Practice listening without interrupting or planning your response. Just be there, fully engaged in what the other person is saying.

2. Mindfulness: Stay present in the moment. Notice your own emotions and thoughts, but don't let them overshadow the person you're connecting with.

3. Compassionate Imagination: Try to imagine what it's like to be in the other person's situation. What might they be feeling? What are their hopes and fears?

4. Non-Judgment: Approach each interaction with an open heart and mind. Let go of any judgments or preconceptions you might have.

Conclusion: The Heartbeat of Oneness

Empathy, dear traveler, is the heartbeat of our shared existence. It's the silent language of the soul, a testament to our interconnectedness. As you cultivate empathy, you deepen your connection not just with others, but with the very fabric of the universe.

So, let's continue this journey with open hearts and minds. Let's embrace each other's stories, feel each other's joys and sorrows, and dance to the rhythm of empathy. In this dance, we find the true essence of our being—together as one, in love and understanding.

May your empathic heart shine brightly, illuminating the path for yourself and others.
And remember, in the grand symphony of life, every note you play adds to the beauty of the whole. Keep playing, keep listening, and keep dancing.

13

❦

The Art of Awareness

Awareness is like the sun. When it shines on things, they are transformed.

Thich Nhat Hanh

The Art of Awareness: Painting with the Light of Consciousness

Welcome back, dear seeker, to another chapter in our exploration of the Self. Having delved into the profound depths of empathy, it's now time to sharpen our focus on the luminous canvas of awareness. Imagine your consciousness as a masterful artist, and awareness as the light that reveals the intricacies of your inner and outer worlds. Let's take up our brushes and paint a vivid portrait of what it means to live with awareness, inspired by the timeless wisdom of Advaita Vedanta, and infused with our signature blend of humor and profundity.

The Spotlight of Consciousness

Awareness, in the tradition of Advaita Vedanta, is the recognition that you are the witnessing presence behind all experiences. It's like sitting in the audience of the grand theater of life, aware of the drama unfolding on stage without being swept away by it. The moment you realize you are not the actor but the observer, the play takes on a whole new dimension.

Picture yourself watching a suspenseful thriller. Your heart races, your palms sweat, but deep down, you know it's just a movie. Similarly, in the theater of life, awareness allows you to observe the highs and lows, the joys and sorrows, without losing your center. It's the art of staying present, come what may.

The Brushstrokes of Presence

Living with awareness is like painting with delicate brushstrokes of presence. It's about bringing your full attention to the here and now, whether you're sipping your morning coffee or navigating a challenging conversation. Each moment becomes an opportunity to practice mindfulness, to be fully engaged with whatever is happening.

Imagine walking through a garden. You could rush through, barely noticing the flowers, or you could stroll mindfully, appreciating the colors, the scents, the textures. When you move through life with awareness, even the mundane becomes magical. The art of awareness transforms every moment into a masterpiece. Today, only meaningful synchronicities exist for me, when I am aware!

The Colors of Non-Duality

Advaita Vedanta teaches us that awareness is the canvas upon which the entire universe is painted. In the vibrant tapestry of existence, every color represents a different aspect of reality, yet all colors emerge from the same source—pure consciousness. When you understand this, you realize that the separation between the observer and the observed is an illusion.

Think of it as looking at a rainbow. At first glance, you see distinct colors, each with its own beauty. But when you delve deeper, you discover that they all arise from the same white light, refracted through the prism of life. Awareness is the white light that reveals the unity behind diversity. Embracing this non-dual perspective brings a profound sense of peace and interconnectedness.

The Play of Shadows and Light

In our journey of awareness, we must also acknowledge the shadows—the parts of ourselves we often avoid or deny. These shadows are not our enemies; they are unpainted areas on our canvas, waiting for the light of awareness to illuminate them. When you shine the light of consciousness on your fears, doubts, and insecurities, you transform them into opportunities for growth and healing.

Imagine a photographer in a darkroom, developing film. The images only become clear when exposed to light. Similarly, our inner shadows reveal their true nature when we face them with awareness. It's in this dance of shadows and light that the full spectrum of our being is revealed.

The Symphony of Silence

At the heart of awareness lies silence—profound, still, and ever-present. This silence is not the absence of sound but the space within which all sounds arise and dissolve. It's the silence of the early morning, the pause between musical notes, the stillness at the center of a storm.

To cultivate awareness, we must learn to embrace this silence. It's in moments of stillness that our true nature is revealed. Take time each day to sit in silence, to listen to the gentle whispers of your soul. In this sacred space, you connect with the infinite, the eternal, the unchanging essence of who you are.

The Joy of Being

As you deepen your practice of awareness, you'll find a profound joy bubbling up from within. This joy is not dependent on external circumstances; it's the natural state of your being. It's the simple plea-sure of being alive, of breathing, of existing.

Think of a child playing in a field, completely absorbed in the moment. This is the joy of awareness—a state of pure, unadulterated presence. When you live with awareness, every moment becomes a celebration, a dance of life unfolding in its perfect harmony.

Conclusion: Masterpieces of Consciousness

As we conclude this chapter on the art of awareness, remember that you are both the artist and the canvas, the creator and the creation. Each moment is an opportunity to paint your life with the colors of presence, to illuminate the shadows with the light of consciousness, and to revel in the symphony of silence.

So, dear traveler, let your awareness be your guide. Embrace each moment with an open heart and a curious mind. Let your life be a masterpiece of consciousness, a testament to the beauty and wonder of existence. And as you continue on this journey, may you find joy, peace, and a deep sense of connection with all that is.

Keep painting, keep observing, and keep shining your light. For in the grand tapestry of life, your awareness is the brightest star, illumi-nating the path for yourself and others.

Messages

by Jody Morrison

There is a little pressure on your arm
a flutter across your hair
and you are sure that pesky fly has
found you again
landing where it doesn't
belong

Coming into the cool
from the sun dazzled snow
you know the shadow that
flits across your vision is a
sunspot
carried in from outdoor sparkles

The number 884 appears
on your phone
your neighbor's license plate
a street sign
a billboard
and you startle and dismiss

There is a perfect circle
of white feathers outside your
back door and the song your best friend
loved to sing, before, is on the radio
five times
on different stations
on the anniversary of his passing

and
that ugly checkered jacket that your dad used to wear is
spotted three times on the street where he used to live.

What more do you want?

Do you want his pipe tobacco smell or
her cologne
or the taste of apple fritters made in granny's kitchen and bacon frying on the
wood stove
and coffee steaming in its cup

we are running
out
of ways to tell you

we are here
we love you
we surround you
we protect you
we want so desperately to
connect with you

But our messages
go
unnoticed
and

we sigh

and plan
our next attempt
to let you know
how much we love you

14

Satori Laughing (@ The Cosmic Joke)

The most wasted of all days is one without laughter.

E.E. Cummings

Satori Laughing: Embracing the Cosmic Joke

Welcome back, fellow traveler, to yet another delightful chapter of our spiritual expedition. We've journeyed through empathy and awareness, and now we arrive at a juncture that brings together wisdom and wit, insight and laughter. It's time to explore Satori—the flash of enlightenment—and how it intertwines with the cosmic joke. So, let's dive into the humor of the universe with the same blend of humor and profundity that has guided us thus far.

The Flash of Enlightenment

In Zen Buddhism, Satori is often described as a sudden flash of insight, a moment where the veil of illusion is lifted, and the truth is revealed. It's the aha moment that transforms your perception, where the ordinary becomes extraordinary. But what makes Satori even more magical is its inherent sense of humor—because the universe loves a good laugh.

Imagine you've been searching high and low for your glasses, only to find them perched on your head the whole time. That's Satori for you—a realization that what you sought was always within you, and the journey itself was a playful, cosmic game.

The Cosmic Joke

At the heart of Satori lies the cosmic joke, the universe's playful reminder not to take life too seriously. The cosmic joke is that life, with all its ups and downs, triumphs and tribulations, is an elaborate play—a divine comedy where you are both the actor and the audience.

Think of it as the ultimate punchline: you've spent years striving, struggling, and seeking, only to discover that you've always been home. It's the moment you laugh out loud at the absurdity of it all, realizing that the joke's on you—and that's perfectly okay.

Laughter: The Sound of Enlightenment

Laughter is the music of enlightenment. When you laugh, you break free from the chains of the ego, the seriousness of the mind, and enter a state of pure, unadulterated presence. Laughter is a direct line to the divine, a spontaneous expression of joy and freedom.

Imagine the Buddha, often depicted with a serene smile. Now, picture him having a good belly laugh. That's the essence of Satori laughing—finding joy in the simplicity of being, in the recognition that all is well, and that the universe is a playful, loving place.

The Humor of Paradox

Satori often comes wrapped in paradox, those delightful contradictions that tickle the mind and expand the heart. It's like a Zen koan—a riddle that defies logic but points to a deeper truth. Embracing paradox is key to understanding the cosmic joke.

Consider this: you are both the wave and the ocean, the individual and the infinite. You strive to become what you already are. The more you seek, the less you find, until you stop seeking and suddenly, there it is. The paradoxes of existence are the universe's way of keeping you on your toes, encouraging you to dance with mystery rather than wrestle with certainty.

Practicing the Art of Cosmic Laughter

How can you cultivate this joyful, enlightened laughter in your daily life? Here are a few practices to tickle your spiritual funny bone:

1. **Embrace Playfulness**: Approach life with a sense of play. Be curious, be spontaneous, and don't be afraid to be a little silly. Playfulness opens the door to Satori.
2. **See the Humor in Your Struggles**: When faced with challenges, try to see the humor in them. Ask yourself, "What's the cosmic joke here?" This shift in perspective can lighten your load and open you to new insights.
3. **Share Laughter with Others**: Laughter is contagious. Share it with friends, family, and even strangers. A shared laugh can create a deep sense of connection and remind you of our shared humanity.
4. **Meditate on Paradox**: Reflect on the paradoxes in your life. Let them percolate in your mind without trying to resolve them. This practice can lead to sudden flashes of insight and, of course, a good laugh.

The Lightness of Being

Satori laughing invites you to experience the lightness of being. It's about letting go of the heavy burdens of judgment, fear, and attachment, and embracing the effervescence of existence. When you laugh with the universe, you rise above the mundane and touch the divine.

Think of a child, laughing with pure delight at the simplest things—a butterfly, a funny face, a splash of water. This childlike wonder is the gateway to Satori. It's a reminder that beneath the layers of conditioning and seriousness, your true nature is joyful and free.

Conclusion: The Ultimate Punchline

As we conclude this chapter on Satori laughing, remember that enlightenment isn't about becoming someone new; it's about realizing who you've always been—a divine being, playing a delightful role in the cosmic theater. The ultimate punchline is that the search for enlightenment ends where it began: right here, right now, in the present moment.

So, dear traveler, keep your heart light, your spirit playful, and your sense of humor intact. Embrace the cosmic joke with open arms and a hearty laugh. For in the grand comedy of life, every moment is an opportunity to experience the joy of Satori, the laughter of enlightenment, and the profound truth that you are already home.

Keep laughing, keep exploring, and keep shining your light. For in the dance of existence, your laughter is the sweetest sound, echoing the joy of the universe itself.

Don't Listen to Me

Take my advice,
Don't listen to me...

Run your own race,
Turnabout's two-faced...

...without love, virtue and grace.

The darkness stands behind me.
You are the light.

Now...
And for all eternity...

But,

Take my advice,
Don't listen to me...

Direct your own play,
Learn and grow...

...your own way.

You are the mirror;
The actors in fusion.

Now...
And for all eternity...

But,

Take my advice,
Don't listen to me...

Throw the confetti,
And, join the party...

...On the Inside.

The song is heart,
Your soul's paternity.

Now...
And for all eternity...

But,

Take my advice,
Don't listen to me...

15

From Aloneness to All-One-ness

Solitude is fine, but you need someone to tell that solitude is fine.

Honoré de Balzac

From Aloneness to All-One-ness: The Journey of Unity

Welcome back, intrepid traveler, to yet another chapter of our shared journey. We've laughed with the universe and embraced the cosmic joke, and now it's time to explore one of the most profound transformations on the spiritual path: the shift from aloneness to all-one-ness. So, settle in, open your heart, and prepare for a journey that is both deeply unifying and surprisingly humorous.

The Illusion of Separation

At some point in our lives, we've all felt the pangs of aloneness—that nagging sense that we are separate from the world around us, isolated in our individual experiences. This feeling can be intense, like standing in a crowded room and still feeling completely alone. But, as Advaita Vedanta teaches us, this sense of separation is an illusion, a trick of the ego.

Imagine life as a grand masquerade ball (yes, we love our ball metaphors!). Each person wears a unique mask, believing they are separate from the others. Yet, when the masks are removed, we see that we are all faces of the same divine being, dancing in unison. The journey from aloneness to all-one-ness is the process of unmasking, of realizing our inherent unity.

The Web of Connection

Advaita Vedanta reminds us that everything is interconnected, like threads in a cosmic tapestry. Each of us is a vital part of this intricate web, and our actions ripple out, affecting the whole. When we shift our perspective from aloneness to all-one-ness, we begin to see these connections everywhere.

Think of it as discovering that you are not a single drop in the ocean, but the entire ocean in a single drop. Your experiences, thoughts, and emotions are part of the vast sea of consciousness. Recognizing this interconnectedness dissolves the illusion of separation and reveals the unity that underlies all existence.

The Heart of Compassion

As we move from aloneness to all-one-ness, we naturally cultivate compassion. When you realize that the pain of another is your own pain, and their joy is your joy, your heart opens wide. Compassion becomes a natural response to the world.

Picture yourself walking through a bustling city. Instead of seeing strangers, you see reflections of yourself—each person carrying a piece of your soul. This realization transforms your interactions, infusing them with kindness and empathy. The barriers of "me" and "you" dissolve, leaving only "us."

The Dance of Oneness

Living in all-one-ness is like participating in a grand dance. Each step, each movement, is synchronized with the cosmic rhythm. There is a profound sense of belonging, of being part of something greater than yourself. This dance of oneness is joyous, vibrant, and full of life.

Imagine a group of dancers moving in perfect harmony. Each one is unique, yet their movements are part of a larger choreography. This is the dance of life in all-one-ness— celebrating diversity while honoring unity.

Embracing Solitude as Sacred

Ironically, embracing all-one-ness often begins with embracing aloneness. Solitude becomes a sacred space, a time to connect deeply with yourself and, through that connection, with the whole. When you are comfortable in your own company, you realize that you are never truly alone.

Think of solitude as a retreat into the heart of existence. In this quiet space, you can hear the whispers of the universe, feel the pulse of life, and reconnect with your true Self. It is here, in the stillness, that you experience the profound truth of all-one-ness.

The Big Twist: The Cosmic Surprise

Now, dear reader, as we reach the climax of this chapter, prepare yourself for a twist that is both profound and delightfully humorous. After all, the universe loves a good laugh.

You've journeyed through life, seeking unity, yearning for that deep connection with all that is. And now, in a moment of meditation, the veil is lifted. You see clearly, with absolute certainty, that you are one with the universe. You are filled with an overwhelming sense of peace and joy.

Then, in a flash of cosmic humor, you hear a gentle chuckle. The universe itself is laughing with you. You look around, puzzled, until you notice something extraordinary. There, sitting right next to you, is a familiar figure—your own reflection. But this time, it's not just your reflection in the mirror. It's a playful, radiant version of you, grinning ear to ear.

"Yes," says your reflection, "the great cosmic joke is this: you've been the universe all along, playing hide and seek with yourself!"

And suddenly, it all makes sense. Every moment of aloneness, every step towards all-one-ness, was a divine game. The seeker and the sought, the dancer and the dance, the knower and the known—they are all you, in myriad forms, laughing at the beautiful simplicity of it all.

Conclusion: The Joyful Union

As we conclude this chapter, let's embrace the profound and humorous truth that we are all expressions of the same divine essence. The journey from aloneness to all-one-ness is a joyous return to our true nature, where we laugh with the universe and celebrate our eternal unity.

So, dear traveler, embrace the dance of oneness, the beauty of connection, and the delightful surprise that you are the universe in disguise. Remember, in the grand cosmic play, we are all one, laughing and loving each other.

Keep smiling, keep dancing, and keep being the beautiful, interconnected being that you are. For in the end, the greatest joke is also the greatest truth: we are all one, and we are all wonderfully, joyfully divine.

Together as One

Into Her arms all will go...
Some will follow...
Others will know.

Touched by Her heart all will grow...
Some will evolve...
Others will show.

And, one by one,
By Her will and grace,
On this plane,
Or in a spiritual place...

We all will rest;

Together as One.

16

An Eternal Present

Time is an illusion. Lunchtime doubly so.

Douglas Adams

Welcome, dear traveler, to the penultimate chapter of our spiritual journey together. We've danced through the realms of empathy, awareness, laughter, and oneness, and now we find ourselves at the doorstep of one of the most intriguing and elusive concepts of all: the eternal present. Prepare for a revelation that will turn your perspective inside out and upside down.

The Illusion of Time

Let's begin with a fundamental truth: time, as we know it, is an illusion. We live our lives bound by the ticking of clocks and the turning of calendars, but these are mere constructs. In reality, there is only the now. Past and future are mental projections, shadows cast by the mind.

Imagine you're watching a film. The events unfold on the screen, but they are all happening in the present moment. The past scenes exist only as memories, and future scenes as expectations. Life is much the same—an ongoing movie where the present moment is the only reality.

The Precious Paradox

Herein lies the precious paradox: while we experience life in a linear fashion, the eternal present is where true reality resides. This paradox can be both perplexing and liberating. It's like finding a hidden room in a house you've lived in all your life. Suddenly, everything is different.

Consider this: a river flows, and while you see it moving from one place to another, the water is always here, now. Similarly, life flows through moments, but the essence of your experience is always anchored in the present. Embracing this paradox can transform how you perceive your existence.

The Art of Presence

Living in the eternal present is an art, one that requires mindfulness and practice. It's about being fully engaged in whatever you are doing, whether it's washing dishes, walking in nature, or having a conversation. Presence brings a richness to life that is incomparable.

Think of a musician playing a beautiful melody. Each note arises and fades in the moment, creating a harmonious flow. The musician isn't lost in thoughts of past performances or future notes; they are immersed in the music of now. This is the essence of presence—being so attuned to the moment that you become the melody itself.

The Freedom of Now

One of the greatest gifts of living in the eternal present is the freedom it brings. When you are fully present, worries about the past and anxieties about the future lose their grip. You are free to experience life in its purest form, unencumbered by the weight of time.

Imagine a child playing in a park, completely absorbed in their game. They are not concerned with what happened yesterday or what will happen tomorrow. They are fully alive in the present moment. This is the freedom of now—a state of being where joy, creativity, and peace naturally arise.

The Big Surprise: The Ultimate Revelation

And now, dear reader, it's time for the twist, the revelation that will shift your perspective forever. As you have journeyed through these chapters, you've uncovered deeper truths about yourself and the universe. Here's the final piece of the puzzle:

In the eternal present, you are not just living life; you are life itself. You are the consciousness experiencing everything, the awareness within which all events unfold. The divine isn't a distant entity; it's the essence of your being, right here, right now.

But here's the kicker, the cosmic punchline that's both funny and profound: you are the divine, and you've been playing a delightful game of hide and seek with yourself all along!

Picture this: you're sitting quietly, meditating on the nature of existence, when suddenly, a thought bubbles up. "What if I am the universe, experiencing itself as me?" You chuckle at the absurdity and profundity of it. And then it hits you—like a thunderbolt of clarity and laughter. The divine is not separate from you; it is you! You've been the seeker and the sought, the question and the answer, the dancer and the dance.

Conclusion: The Dance of Life

As we conclude this chapter, let's celebrate this magnificent revelation. Life is a dance, and you are both the dancer and the dance. The eternal present is your stage, where every moment is an opportunity to express your divine nature, to laugh at the cosmic joke, and to revel in the joy of existence.

So, dear traveler, keep your heart open, your spirit playful, and your awareness anchored in the now. Embrace the precious paradox of the eternal present, and let your life be a testament to the beauty, humor, and profound unity of the universe.

And remember, in the grand play of life, you are not just an actor; you are the playwright, the director, and the audience. You are the divine experiencing itself in myriad forms, and every moment is a new act in the greatest comedy of all.

Keep laughing, keep loving, and keep shining your light. For in the end, the greatest surprise is also the greatest truth: you are the universe, and the universe is you, dancing together in the eternal present.

As within, so without

Within the heart's silent chamber, a light does softly dwell,
A spark of the divine, in this earthly shell.

It whispers of a truth, that's both ancient and forever new,
That within each of us, the universe does gently brew.

Beyond the skin's soft boundary, the cosmos grandly lies,
A tapestry of stars, draped across the skies.

The divine dances there, in every leaf and stone,
In the vastness of the void, we are never truly alone.

The inner light, it guides us, through the dark and unknown,
A compass of the soul, pointing to where love has grown.

And the outer glow, it beckons, with a promise wide and deep,

That the sacred is all around us, for us to sense and keep.

So, look within, and marvel, at the mystery you contain,
And gaze out, with wonder, at the world's majestic plane.

For the divine is both the journey, and the destination clear,
In the quiet of your spirit, and the universe's grand frontier.

By Jeff Malderez & A. Nobody

17

The Phoenix and the Magic of Rebirth

And the day came when the risk to remain tight in a bud was more pain-ful than the risk it took to blossom.

Anaïs Nin

In a land where the mystical and the mundane intertwined, there lived a Phoenix, a majestic bird of radiant plumage, whose feathers shimmered with the colors of dawn and dusk. This Phoenix was unlike any other, for it embodied the essence of both the spiritual and the tangible realms. Its life was a perpetual cycle of death and rebirth, symbolizing the eternal dance of transformation and enlightenment.

The Beginning of the Journey

Once, in a serene valley nestled between ancient mountains, a young seeker named Aria lived. She was a curious soul, always in search of deeper truths and the meaning behind life's mysteries. Aria had heard tales of the Phoenix, the legendary bird that could teach one the secrets of existence and the art of rising from the ashes.

Determined to find the Phoenix, Aria embarked on a journey, guided by whispers of the wind and the light of the stars. She traveled through dense forests, crossed turbulent rivers, and climbed rugged mountains, facing numerous challenges that tested her spirit and resolve. With each trial, Aria grew stronger and more aware of her inner strength, yet she still felt an aching sense of aloneness.

The Encounter

One twilight, as Aria reached the summit of a sacred mountain, she saw a brilliant burst of light on the horizon. Drawn to it, she discovered the Phoenix perched atop a solitary peak, its feathers glowing with an ethereal fire. The Phoenix's eyes, filled with ancient wisdom and playful humor, met Aria's gaze.

"Welcome, seeker," the Phoenix said in a voice that resonated like the melody of the cosmos. "You have traveled far and faced many trials. What is it that you seek?"

"I seek the truth," Aria replied. "I seek to understand the mysteries of life, death, and rebirth. I wish to know how to rise from my own ashes."

The Lesson

The Phoenix nodded, its eyes twinkling. "To understand the cycle of life and rebirth, you must first embrace the paradox of existence. Life is a journey from aloneness to all-one- ness, from seeking to realizing that what you seek has always been within you."

The Phoenix began to weave a tale, a parable of sorts:

"In the heart of the universe lies a magical fire, the source of all creation. From this fire, everything is born, and to this fire, everything returns. This cycle is the essence of the Phoenix, the eternal dance of transformation.

Once, there was a young Phoenix who felt a deep sense of isolation, believing itself to be separate from the world. It flew across the heavens, seeking the secret of its existence, yearning to understand its place in the grand tapestry of life. One day, exhausted and disheartened, it descended into a forest, where it met an ancient tree, wise and rooted in the earth.

The tree said to the Phoenix, 'You search for answers in the vastness of the sky, but the truth lies within you. You are not just a single flame; you are the fire itself. Embrace your inner light, and you will find that you are connected to all things.'

The Phoenix, pondering these words, realized the profound truth. In a moment of clarity, it allowed itself to be consumed by its own flames, surrendering to the process of transformation. From its ashes, it rose anew, not as a separate being, but as a living embodiment of the eternal fire."

The Revelation

As the Phoenix concluded its tale, Aria felt a surge of understanding and joy. She realized that her journey mirrored that of the Phoenix. The trials she faced were not just obstacles but opportunities to awaken to her true nature. The sense of aloneness she felt was an illusion; in reality, she was part of the infinite web of life, connected to everything and everyone.

With a smile, the Phoenix said, "Remember, dear Aria, the magic of rebirth lies within you. Each moment is an opportunity to rise from your ashes, to embrace the eternal present, and to live in the light of awareness. The universe is a grand play, and you are both the actor and the audience, the dancer and the dance."

The Return

Aria returned to her village, carrying the wisdom of the Phoenix in her heart. She no longer sought answers outside herself, for she understood that the journey of life was about realizing the divine within. She lived each day with a sense of joy, compassion, and presence, sharing her newfound insights with others.

The tale of the Phoenix spread far and wide, inspiring many to embark on their own journeys of transformation. And so, the magic of the Phoenix continued, a timeless dance of life, death, and rebirth, reminding all who listened that they, too, had the power to rise from their ashes and embrace the light of the eternal present.

In the end, dear reader, remember this: You are the Phoenix, and the fire of rebirth burns brightly within you. Embrace your journey with humor and wisdom, knowing that you are never alone. For in the grand tapestry of existence, we are all one, eternally connected, and infinitely divine.

As far as I can tell, the real joy of life is in the unknown, a divine self-forgetting ... And a glorious re-awakening and remembering of the infinite existence of us all as One...

...now, and all-ways!

Jeff Malderez & A. Nobody (2024)

Referenced Publications

- Alcoholics Anonymous, (2004). Twelve Steps and Twelve Traditions. New York: Alcoholics Anonymous World Services Inc.
- Campbell, J. (1988). The power of myth. New York: Broadway Books.
- Campbell, J. (1991). A Joseph Campbell Companion: Reflections on the Art of Living. San Anselmo, CA: The Joseph Campbell Foundation.
- Crowley, N. (2006). 'Psychosis or Spiritual Emergence? - Consideration of the Transpersonal Perspective within Psychiatry.' www.rcpsych.ac.uk
- Lajoie, D. & Shapiro, S. I. (1992). Definitions of transpersonal psychology: The first 23 years. The Journal of Transpersonal Psychology, 24(1), 79-98.
- Szasz, T. S. (1973). The second sin. Garden City, NY: Anchor/Doubleday.
- Cortright, B. (1997). Psychotherapy and Spirit. Albany, NY: State University of New York Press.
- Grof, C., & Grof, S. (1986). Spiritual emergency: The understanding and treatment of transpersonal crises. ReVision, Vol. 8, (No. 2), 7-20.
- Grof, C. & Grof, S. (1990). The Stormy Search for the Self: Understanding and Living with Spiritual Emergency. Los Angeles, CA: Jeremy P Tarcher Inc.
- Harper, D. J. (2004). Delusions and discourse: Moving beyond the constraints of the rationalist paradigm. Philosophy, Psychiatry & Psychology, 11, 55-64.
- May, R. (2010). Accepting Alternative Realities. www.rufusmay.com
- Walsh, R. & Vaughan, F. (1993). On Transpersonal Definitions. Journal of Transpersonal Psychology, Vol. 25, (No. 2), 199-207.
- Peters, E. R., Joseph, S. A. & Garety, P. (1999). Measurement of delusional ideation in the normal population: Introducing the PDI (Peters et al. Delusions Inventory). Schizophrenia Bulletin, 25, 553-576.

Silhouettes

A white mist sweeps across
My field of vision,
An image,
Of static transmission...

And yet,
The voice is clear...

"That cross is not yours to bear.

Silhouettes...
Is what they are"

This being a message from your Grandpa.

Here today and gone the next,
Silhouettes...

Place your bets.

Ashes to ashes,
Dust to dust,

"Play your hand boy...

Go for bust!"